Classroom English Handbook

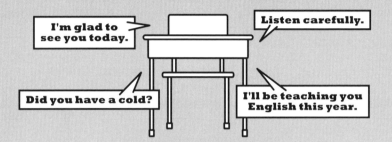

教室英語
ハンドブック

高梨庸雄　小野尚美　土屋佳雅里　田縁眞弓
編

研究社

はしがき

英語は、学校教育において最も活発に改革が試みられてきた教科の1つであろう。2015年は「戦後70年」の年として知られるが、英語教育の70年はつねに「改革」の掛け声とともにあった。しかしその成果はどうだろうか。英語教育の成果を測る1つの尺度として、CEFR（ヨーロッパ言語共通参照枠）の英語能力6段階のスケール（A1, A2: B1, B2: C1, C2）を参照すると、日本人英語学習者の多くはA（基礎段階）にとどまっているという。なぜだろうか。

その理由は単純ではないが、1つには、改革・改善というアドバルーンは上げても、それを草の根レベルから着実に実行すること、つまり、実際に生徒を教え導くべき教師たちへの支援、研修の不足が挙げられるのではないだろうか。たとえば教育職員免許法施行規則によると、英語教員になるために教員養成課程で修得すべき科目とその単位数は、教科に関する科目20単位、教職に関する科目8単位で、その内訳は「英語学」、「英米文学」、「英語コミュニケーション」、「異文化理解」という各科目に関して1単位以上計20単位である（一種免許状。専修免許状の場合は一種免許状の必要単位数に加えて教科又は教職に関する科目でさらに24単位)。これはかなり大雑把な内容であり、極端な場合は教科4科目については、特定の1科目で16単位、残りの4単位を他の科目で履修することも理論上は可能である。

その結果、教壇に立った際に本当に必要な能力や技術が不足したまま教員志望者が教師になってしまう状況が生まれる。指導に必要な能力や技術は、新採用教員研修で一定のレベルまで向上して足並みがそろうほど生易しいものではないのだ。一方、教員はますます多忙になり、日々の授業の準備の時間を確保するのも容易ではない。このような中で新しい教育政策が施行されれば、一番苦労するのは現場の教師である。これは避けなければならない。本書は、このような視点から、現場の先生方のお仕事を少しでもスムーズに履行できるようにと願って編集されたものである。

本書の母体は『教室英語活用事典』（研究社）である。おかげさま

で、多くの読者に歓迎され、1992 年 7 月に初版を刊行してから 2004 年 7 月の改訂版発行を経て、23 年間お使いいただいている。執筆に関係された方々に改めて感謝申し上げたい。近年、小学校における「外国語活動」が必修になり、開始学年も早まることが想定され、小中の連携がさらに重要になる。そこで『教室英語ハンドブック』の名称で、より使いやすくわかりやすいものを刊行することになった。今回特に留意したのは次の 5 点である。

1. 多忙な教員の現状に配慮し、各ページの左側に日本語、右側に英語を配置し、必要な表現がすぐわかるようにした。
2. 「外国語活動」の必修化並びに予想される開始学年の早期化に対応するため、小学校英語関連のページを大幅に増やした。
3. 児童・生徒の情意教育の重要性に鑑み、Storytelling に関するページを設けた。
4. 小中連携のためのページを新設し、オーラル・コミュニケーションの表現や小中連携を意識した授業モデルを掲載した。
5. 例文の英語の音声を native speakers に録音してもらい、研究社のホームページから利用できるようにした。

本書は『教室英語活用事典』の豊富な例文を資料として活用させていただいた。『教室英語活用事典（改訂版）』の編者である髙梨庸雄、高橋正夫、カール・アダムズ、久埜百合の各氏にお礼申し上げる。この事典は今後も継続して販売される。

研究社の津田正、大谷千明、杉本義則の三氏には編集のいろいろな段階でお世話になった。その貴重なご助言のおかげで、見やすく使いやすいハンドブックになった。心から感謝申し上げる次第である。

2015 年 11 月

編　者

目次
Contents

はしがき iii
本書の使い方 xii
音声のダウンロード方法 xiv

I 小学校英語 1
Classroom English in Elementary School

Chapter 1 2
基本的な指示をするとき

Chapter 2 7
動きの指示をするとき
　ア．動きの指示をする 7
　イ．ポーズを指示する 9
　ウ．位置を指示する 11
　エ．順番を決める 11

Chapter 3 13
活動をするとき
　ア．ペア、グループを作る 13
　イ．カードを使って活動する 14
　ウ．カルタ・すごろくをする 15
　エ．ゲームをする 16

Chapter 4 18
作業・制作活動をするとき
　ア．紙を用いる活動をする 18
　イ．道具を使う 18
　ウ．絵・図を描く 19

Chapter 5 21
演じる活動をするとき

Chapter 6 22
クイズ・歌の活動をするとき
　ア．クイズの活動をする 22
　イ．歌う活動をする 22

Chapter 7 24
DVD・ビデオや絵本・紙芝居などを観るとき

Chapter 8 25
ストーリー・テリング
①絵本の読み聞かせ法 25
　a 絵本を開く前に 25
　b 読み聞かせ 26
　c 読後活動 28

②ストーリー・テリング 29
　a お話 29
　b お話タイム 29
　c お話の仕方 30
　d お話のための質問 30
　e 確認用質問 30
　f 話題 31
　g 読みに誘う 32

II 一般的指示
General Directions ... 33

Chapter 1 ... 34
移動
- ⓐ 席の移動 ... 34
- ⓑ 教室内（から）の移動 ... 35

Chapter 2 ... 36
注目
- ⓐ 板書に ... 36
- ⓑ 生徒に ... 36
- ⓒ 教師に ... 37
- ⓓ 参観者に ... 37
- ⓔ 図・絵に ... 38
- ⓕ 窓の外に ... 39

Chapter 3 ... 40
起立・着席
- ⓐ 起立 ... 40
  - ア．個人で ... 40
  - イ．列・班ごとに ... 40
  - ウ．ペアで ... 41
  - エ．全員で ... 41
- ⓑ 着席 ... 42
  - ア．個人で ... 42
  - イ．複数人で ... 42

Chapter 4 ... 43
注意・叱責
- ⓐ 静かに ... 43
  - ア．クラス全体に ... 43
  - イ．個々の生徒に ... 43
- ⓑ 顔を上げて ... 44
- ⓒ 私語の禁止 ... 44
  - ア．最初の注意 ... 44
  - イ．（注意してもやめないので）しかる ... 44
- ⓓ いたずらの禁止 ... 45
  - ア．短い注意 ... 45
  - イ．長めの注意 ... 45
- ⓔ その他の注意 ... 45

Chapter 5 ... 46
発言
- ⓐ 大きな声で（言う・話す）... 46
- ⓑ もっとはっきりと ... 46
- ⓒ 口を大きく開けて ... 47
- ⓓ 意味を考えて ... 47
- ⓔ 発言を促す ... 48
  - ア．答えを促す ... 48
  - イ．質問を受ける ... 48
- ⓕ 挙手 ... 49

Chapter 6 ... 50
ほめる
- ⓐ 一般的なほめ言葉 ... 50
- ⓑ 声の質 ... 50
- ⓒ 声の大きさ ... 51
- ⓓ 努力 ... 51
  - ア．成果に対して ... 51
  - イ．ねぎらう ... 52
- ⓔ 手書きの文字 ... 52
- ⓕ 向上の度合い ... 52
- ⓖ 試験の結果 ... 53

Chapter 7 ... 54
励まし
- ⓐ 希望をもたせる ... 54
- ⓑ 意欲をかき立てる ... 54
- ⓒ 積極性を引き出す ... 55
- ⓓ 好調を持続させる ... 55
- ⓔ 慰め・同情 ... 56
- ⓕ 生徒の応答を励ます ... 56

Chapter 8 ... 57
あやまる
- **a** 遅刻して ... 57
  - ア．教師が遅れて教室に入る ... 57
  - イ．理由の説明 ... 57
- **b** 生徒の釈明に対して ... 58
- **c** 予告なしの自習のあとで ... 58
- **d** 宿題が多すぎて ... 58
- **e** 勘違いして ... 59
- **f** 急用で授業を中座して ... 59
  - ア．教師の発言 ... 59
  - イ．生徒の発言 ... 59

Chapter 9 ... 60
感謝
- **a** 一般的な「ありがとう」 ... 60
- **b** 手伝いに対して ... 60
  - ア．手伝いを頼む ... 60
  - イ．生徒が手伝いを申し出る ... 61
  - ウ．手伝いに感謝する ... 61
- **c** 掃除 ... 61
  - ア．掃除の指示 ... 61
  - イ．掃除に感謝 ... 62
- **d** 花などに対して ... 63
- **e** プレゼントに対して ... 63

Chapter 10 ... 64
生徒の発言への対応
- **a** 誤りの訂正 ... 64
  - ア．誤りを指摘する ... 64
  - イ．小さな[大きな]誤り ... 64
- **b** 場面ごとの誤りの訂正 ... 65
  - ア．音声 ... 65
  - イ．文法 ... 65
  - ウ．綴り字・句読法 ... 66
- **c** 理解の確認 ... 67
- **d** 任意参加を求める ... 67
- **e** 指名して反応を喚起 ... 68
  - ア．指名 ... 68
  - イ．反応を促す ... 68
  - ウ．助け舟を出して ... 68
- **f** 無反応の状況で ... 69

Chapter 11 ... 70
学習活動への指示
- **a** グループワーク ... 70
- **b** ペアワーク ... 70
- **c** 聞くこと ... 71
- **d** 読むこと ... 72
- **e** 文法 ... 72
- **f** 語彙 ... 73
- **g** 子どもたちの活動 ... 74

III 授業展開 ... 75
Teaching Procedure

Chapter 1 ... 76
ウォームアップ
① 挨拶 ... 76
- **a** 挨拶 ... 76
  - ア．普段の挨拶 ... 76
  - イ．休み明けの挨拶 ... 77
- **b** 生徒の反応に続けて ... 78
- **c** 時間 ... 79
- **d** 曜日・月日 ... 80
- **e** 自己紹介 ... 80
  - ア．教師から ... 80
  - イ．生徒に自己紹介を促す ... 81

② 出欠・遅刻 ... 82
- **a** 出席の確認 ... 82
- **b** 欠席[遅刻]の理由 ... 83
  - ア．欠席の理由 ... 83
  - イ．遅刻の理由 ... 83
  - ウ．注意 ... 84
- **c** 健康状態を気遣う ... 85

- ③ 天候 86
  - ⓐ 晴れ 86
  - ⓑ 曇り 86
  - ⓒ 雨 87
  - ⓓ 暖かい 87
  - ⓔ 暑い 88
  - ⓕ 蒸し暑い 88
  - ⓖ 寒い 89
  - ⓗ 霜・氷 90
  - ⓘ 雪 90
- ④ 前日〔先週〕の話題 91
  - ⓐ 普段の生活 91
    - ア．家庭生活 91
    - イ．学校生活 91
    - ウ．社会生活 92
  - ⓑ 週の始め・休暇明け 93
  - ⓒ 週の終わり頃 94

Chapter 2 95
復習

- ① 宿題の提出 95
  - ⓐ 係が集める 95
  - ⓑ 列ごとに集める 96
  - ⓒ 教卓に出す 96
  - ⓓ 授業後に提出 97
- ② 宿題の発表 97
  - ⓐ 口頭で 97
  - ⓑ 板書で 98
  - ⓒ 隣の人と宿題チェック 98
- ③ 暗唱文の確認 99
  - ⓐ 口頭英作文として 99
  - ⓑ 対話形式で 99
  - ⓒ 一人で 100
  - ⓓ 意味を考えて 100
  - ⓔ 気持ちを込めて 101
- ④ 前時のテキスト 102
  - ⓐ 要約 102
  - ⓑ 主人公の行動 102
  - ⓒ 対話の理解 103

Chapter 3 104
導入

- ① 重要構文 104
  - ⓐ 意味 104
    - ア．日本語で意味をとらえさせる ... 104
    - イ．聞いてその文の内容を考えさせる
    104
  - ⓑ 表現形式 105
  - ⓒ 読み方 105
  - ⓓ 言い換え 106
- ② 演示による導入 106
  - ⓐ 教師の動作 106
  - ⓑ 生徒の動作 107
  - ⓒ 動作の指示 107
  - ⓓ ２つの動作の相違 108
  - ⓔ 役割指定 108
    - ア．役割を教師が指定 108
    - イ．グループ内で生徒同士が役割決定
    108
- ③ 新出語 109
  - ⓐ 発音 109
  - ⓑ 意味 109
    - ア．実物を使って 109
    - イ．絵を使って 109
    - ウ．英語で 109
  - ⓒ フラッシュカードで 110
  - ⓓ 連語 110
  - ⓔ 同音異義語 111
- ④ 本文・対話 111
  - ⓐ 要点 111
  - ⓑ 質問 111
  - ⓒ 登場人物の相互関係 112

Chapter 4 113
練習

- ① 語と文 113
  - ⓐ 強勢 113
  - ⓑ イントネーション 113
  - ⓒ 例文 114

ix

d ルックアップ・アンド・セイ 114
　　　e 綴り 115

② 文型練習 116
　　a 代入 116
　　b 語順転換 116
　　c 文転換 116
　　d 拡大 117
　　e 短縮 117

③ 動作を伴う練習 117
　　a TPR 117
　　b ジャズ・チャンツ 118

④ 練習の指示 119
　　a 個人、班ごとの切り替え 119
　　b ノートの取り方・板書の写し方 120
　　c 図・絵などの説明 120

⑤ 書く作業 120
　　a プリントの配布 120
　　b ワークブック 121
　　c OHP で 121
　　d 筆記体・活字体 122
　　e なぐり書き・丁寧に書く 123
　　f ペン・鉛筆 123
　　g 色を塗る 123
　　h 図を描く 124

⑥ 黒板での作業 124
　　a チョーク [マーカー] の指示 124
　　b 板書の指示 125
　　c 下線を引く 125
　　d 板書を消す 126

Chapter 5 127
教科書本文

① 読み方 127
　　a 範読 127
　　b 教師のあとについて読む 127
　　c CD のあとについて読む 128
　　d 音読 129
　　e 黙読 129

　　f 個人読み 130
　　　ア．みんなに向けて読む場合 130
　　　イ．生徒が各自で読む場合 130
　　g ペア読み 131
　　h 斉読 131
　　i 読む箇所の指定 132
　　j イントネーション 132
　　k 強勢 133
　　l 発音の訂正 133

② 内容把握 134
　　a 語 [句・文] の意味 134
　　b 段落の大意 135
　　　ア．大意把握の指示 135
　　　イ．大意把握の具体的方法 135
　　c 指示語の把握 136
　　d 和訳 136
　　　ア．和訳の指示 136
　　　イ．和訳をよくしようとする場合 136
　　e パラフレーズ 137

③ 文法練習 138
　　a 書き換え 138
　　b 和文英訳 138
　　　ア．和文英訳の指示 138
　　　イ．誤りを訂正する場合 139
　　　ウ．別の訳を検討する場合 139
　　c 穴埋め 139
　　d 文の転換・結合 140
　　　ア．文の転換 140
　　　イ．文の結合 141

④ 言語活動 141
　　a 聞くこと 141
　　b 話すこと 142
　　c 読むこと 143
　　d 書くこと 143

Chapter 6 144
終了

① 残り時間 144
　　a 残り時間が短い場合 144
　　　ア．急いで進む 144

- イ．生徒を呼び止めて 145
- ⓑ 残り時間が長い場合 145
  - ア．予定外の活動を入れる 145
  - イ．早めに終わる 146
- ⓒ 予定の変更 146
- ⓓ 次回の予告 147
- ⓔ チャイム 148

② 宿題の指示 148
- ⓐ 教科書の該当箇所 148
  - ア．宿題の指示 148
  - イ．指示の確認 149
- ⓑ 暗唱文の指定 149

- ⓒ 単語・句の確認 149
  - ア．予習 149
  - イ．練習 150
- ⓓ プリント 150
- ⓔ 小テストの予告 151

③ 終わりの挨拶 151
- ⓐ 一般的な挨拶 151
- ⓑ 来週まで 152
- ⓒ 次時まで間が空く場合 152
- ⓓ 長期休暇の前 152
- ⓔ 時間割変更の予告 153
- ⓕ 休講の予告 153
- ⓖ あと片づけ 154

IV 小中連携のためのヒント 155
Hints for Cooperation between Elementary and Junior High Schools

Chapter 1 157
オーラル・コミュニケーション

- ⓐ 日常会話 157
  - ア．授業前にリラックスさせる 157
  - イ．自分のことを話させる 157
  - ウ．ペアで活動させる 158
  - エ．グループで活動させる 159
- ⓑ リスニング 159
  - ア．オーディオ機器を使う 159
  - イ．教師が音読して聞かせる 160
  - ウ．作業を行わせる 161
- ⓒ スピーチ・討論 162
  - ア．意見を求める 162
  - イ．スピーチをさせる 162
  - ウ．暗唱させる 163
  - エ．討論をさせる 164

Chapter 2 165
小中連携を意識した タスク活動例

- タスク活動例①
  英語で時間を聞き、英語で答える 165
- タスク活動例②
  学校の周辺にある店を英語で言う 169
- 小タスク活動例①
  英語でクイズに挑戦！スリーヒント・クイズ 170
- 小タスク活動例②
  英語で時間割を言ってみよう！ 172
- 小中連携を意識した指導のポイント 173

本書の使い方

本書の構成

全4部構成。

第1部 「小学校英語」では、小学校で使われることを想定した教室英語を収録。例文だけでなく、ジェスチャー、指導の際の注意点や Storytelling の具体的な進め方についても解説した。

第2部 「一般的指示」は指導過程のどの段階においても、かなり頻繁に使う教室英語を集めた。

第3部 「授業展開」は授業をする際に必要な教室英語をおおむね指導過程に従って配列した。

第4部 「小中連携のためのヒント」では、教室英語を用いた授業の例として「オーラル・コミュニケーション」「小中連携を意識したタスク活動例」を紹介している。

本書で使われる記号

[ ]　直前の語句と置き換えられることを示す。意味が変わらない場合と，変わる場合がある。

例：・Take [Draw] one.（1枚取ってください）
　　・Face the front [the board].（前［黒板のほう］を向きましょう）
　　・Stand by [in front of] your desk.（机のそばに［前に］立ちなさい）
　　・What beautiful handwriting this is [you have]!（この字は［あなたの字は］とてもきれいです）

( )　カッコ内の語句が省略可能であることを示す。

例：・(Go) back to your seat.（席に戻りなさい）
　　・Thank you (very much).（ありがとう）
　　・Clean up your desk(s).（机を片付けて）

/　例文、表現を並列する。

例：・Hello again, class. / Welcome back, everyone!（皆さん、またよろしく）
　　・Good morning, class [everybody / everyone / boys and girls / students].（皆さん、おはようございます）
　　・Work in pairs [threes / fours].（2人で［3人で、4人で］やりなさい）

⇒　参照ページを示す。

タイトルは、その例文が使われる状況を示している。

ダウンロード音声のフォルダ番号と、該当の音声が何番目のトラックに入っているかを示している。

Classroom English Handbook

Chapter 1 移動
Movement

a 席の移動　Changing seats

TRACK 02 01

1.	座りなさい。	Sit down.
2.	早く座って。	Take your seats quickly.
3.	自分の席に戻って。	Go (back) to your seat.
4.	立ち上がって動き回りなさい。	Stand up and move around.
5.	自由に動き回ってもいいですよ。	You are free to move around.
6.	質問に答えられる人を見つけなさい。	Find someone who can answer the questions.
7.	隣の人と対面しなさい。	Stand face to face with your neighbor [partner].
8.	聞きたいことを誰に聞いてもいいよ。	You may ask anyone, anything you like.
9.	よし、班ごとに作業。	OK, let's make [get into] groups.
10.	好きなように3人の班になって。	Get into groups of three as you like.

英語の例文と英語タイトルの音声を収録。例文の切り替わりがわかりやすいよう、男性の声と女性の声が交互に吹き込まれている。

生徒の応答 Student Response

席を離れていい？	Can we leave our seats now?
今日の席はいつもと同じ？	Is today's seating as usual?
席替えしてほしい。	We want a new seating order.

日本語（左）と英語（右）を一目で対照できる。

「生徒の応答」「教師と生徒のやりとり」では、そのセクションに関連する生徒の発話の例を紹介した。生徒が英語を発話する際の参考として教えてもよいだろう。

音声のダウンロード方法

　本書の例文の英語音声は、研究社のホームページ（**http://www.kenkyusha.co.jp/**）から、無料でダウンロードいただけます（MP3 データ）。以下の手順でダウンロードしてください。

1) 研究社ホームページのトップページで「音声ダウンロード」をクリックして「音声データダウンロード書籍一覧」のページに移動してください。

2) 移動したページの「教室英語ハンドブック」の紹介欄に「ダウンロード」ボタンがあります。クリックしていただくと、ファイルのダウンロードが始まります。

3) ダウンロード完了後、解凍してお使いください。本書の TRACK 番号のアイコンの表示にしたがって、該当するフォルダ・番号の MP3 音声をお使いください。

研究社のホームページ
http://www.kenkyusha.co.jp/ 　研究社　検索

ダウンロードアイコンの見方

| フォルダ番号を示す | ((• TRACK 01 28 •)) | フォルダ内での番号を示す |

ダウンロード音声のフォルダ一覧

- フォルダ **1**　Ⅰ　小学校英語
- フォルダ **2**　Ⅱ　一般的指示
- フォルダ **3**　Ⅲ　授業展開 Chapter1 〜 3
- フォルダ **4**　Ⅲ　授業展開 Chapter4 〜 6
- フォルダ **5**　Ⅳ　小中連携のためのヒント
- フォルダ **6**　タイトル、ナレーター情報

Classroom English
Handbook

小学校英語

Classroom English in
Elementary School

基本的な指示をするとき

Classroom Management

TRACK 01 01

1. 皆さん、いますか？   Is everyone here?
2. よく聞きましょう。   Listen carefully.
   ＊Notes ①

↑ 耳に手を当てて、じっと聞くしぐさ

3. よく見てください。   Look carefully.
   ＊Notes ②

↑ 手を双眼鏡に見立てて、じっと見るしぐさ

4. 本［教科書］の 20 ページを見てください。   Look at page 20 in your book.

Chapter 1 | 基本的な指示をするとき

5. 本［教科書］の 20 ペー
   ジを開いてください。

   Open your book [textbook] to page 20.

   ↑ 両手を本に見立ててパタンと開く

6. 本［教科書］を閉じま
   しょう。

   Close your book [textbook].

   ↑ 開いた両手をパタンと閉じる

7. 1 枚取ってください。

   Take [Draw] one.

8. 後ろ［次］の人に送っ
   てください。

   Pass them down [on].

   ＊pass around 〜は「順に回す」の意味。

9. もっと、はっきり言っ
   てください。

   Speak more clearly, please.

10.	静かにしなさい。	Be quiet. / Shhhh...

↑ Shhhh（シーっ）と言いながら

11.	用意はいいですか？	Ready? / Are you ready?
12.	質問はありますか？	Any questions?
13.	終わりです。	Time is up. / Stop.
14.	英語で（言いましょう、書きましょう）。	In English, please.
15.	大丈夫ですか？	Are you OK [all right]?
16.	大丈夫ですよ。	That's OK.
17.	もっと大きな声で言いましょう。	Louder, please. / Speak up.

↑ 口を大きく開け、手も同様に大きく広げる

18.	あとに続いて言って［やって］ください。	Follow me.

19.	もう一回言ってください。	Say it again.

↑「もう1回」のジェスチャー

20.	もう一回やってみてください。	Try again.
21.	続けてください。	Go on. / Go ahead.
22.	さあ、がんばって。	Come on. Try it.
23.	よくできました！	Good job!
24.	大きな拍手をしましょう。	Let's give a big hand.

↑ 拍手を促す

25.	今日はこれで終わりです。	That's all for today.
26.	さようなら。また次回［来週］会いましょう。	Bye. See you next time [week].

27. よい週末を！　　　　　　**Have a nice weekend!**

Notes: ①ジェスチャーもつけて
　英語を発話する際は、理解を助けるジェスチャーを一緒に使うと効果的。本書では、いくつかの表現にジェスチャーの例を付けて掲載した。

Notes: ② see / look / watch を使い分けよう
　see / look /watch のように、日本語では同じ表現に見えても、使い分けが必要な場合がある。
　see: 意識しなくても自然と視界に入るとき。
　look: 意識して静止しているものを見るとき。
　watch: 意識して動いているもの・変化するものを見たりするとき。

Chapter 2 動きの指示をするとき

Directing Students' Actions

ア．動きの指示をする Directing Students' Actions

((• TRACK 01 02 •))

1. じっとして。　　　　　Stand [Sit] still.

2. 動かないで。　　　　　Don't move. / Freeze.

3. さがってください。　　Move back(ward).

↑ 手で動きを示す

4. ぐるっと回ってください。　　Turn around.

↑ 指でぐるっと回る様子を示す

5. 前［黒板のほう］を向きましょう。　　Face the front [the board].

6. 後ろを向いてください。　Turn around. / Face the back.

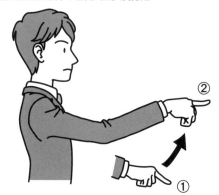

↑ 指で後ろを向くよう指示する

7. 私のまねをしてください。　Do as I do. / Copy me.

↑ この動作のあと、まねさせたい動作を示す

8. 私の言う通りにしてくださいね。　Do what I say.

9. こうですよ。　(Do it) like this.

10. そうではなく、こうです。　Not like that, but like this.

11. 友達の肩［背中］をポ　　Tap your friend on the shoulder [the back].
　　ンとたたいてください。

↑肩（または背中）をたたく動作をしながら友達を手で示す

イ．ポーズを指示する　Indicating How to Pause

((・ TRACK 01 03 ・))

1. 右手を挙げてください。　　**Raise your right hand.**
2. 右足を上げてください。　　**Lift your right leg.**
3. 片足で立ってください。　　**Stand on one leg.**

↑動作を示して児童にまねさせる

4. 両手を前に出してください。　Put both your hands in front.

5. 両手を挙げてください。　Raise both your hands.

6. 腕を左右に伸ばしてください。　Spread your arms wide.

7. 目を閉じて［開けて］ください。　Close [Open] your eyes.

8. 向かい合ってください。　Face each other.

↑ お互いに顔を合わせることを示す

9. 友達の手を取ってください。　Hold your friend's hand.

↑ ①友達を手で指し示す　　↑ ②自分の両手を握る

10. 足首を押さえてください。　Hold your ankles.

Chapter 2 | 動きの指示をするとき

11. 膝にさわってください。 Touch your knees.

Notes:「動作の指示」p.107、「TPR」p.117 も参照。

ウ．位置を指示する　Indicating Directions   TRACK 01 04

1. 位置について。用意。ドン！ On your mark. Get set. Go!
2. 私から見えるところに座ってください。 Sit where I can see you.
3. 黒板の前に立ってください。 Stand in front of the blackboard [the board].
4. 後ろ向きで立ってください。 Stand with your back toward me.
5. どこでも座っていいですよ。 You can sit anywhere you like.
6. 窓［ドア］の近くに立ってください。 Stand by the window [the door].
7. 教室の後ろへ行ってください。 Go to the back of the room.
8. 壁のほうを向いてください。 Face the wall.

エ．順番を決める　Deciding Orders   TRACK 01 05

1. 最初は誰がやりますか［やってみますか、話しますか］？ Who goes [tries / speaks, etc.] first?
2. 一番にやりたい人はいますか？ Who wants to try first?

3.	じゃんけんで順番を決めましょう。グー、チョキ、パー！	Do "*Janken*" to decide the order. Rock, scissors, paper, one, two, three!
4.	コインで決めましょう。	Let's toss a coin.
5.	表ですか、裏ですか？	Heads or tails?
6.	かわりばんこで。	Take turns.
7.	自分の番まで待ってください。	Wait for your turn.
8.	割り込みはだめですよ。	Don't cut in.
9.	役を交替してください。	Switch the roles.

Notes: please を付けて丁寧な表現に

　please を用いると丁寧な表現に。相手に対して丁寧な表現を使うことを指南するため、子どもたちにも please をつけて指示したい。

Chapter 3 活動をするとき
Activities

ア．ペア、グループを作る Making Pairs or Groups　　TRACK 01 06

1.	ペアになってください。	Make pairs.
2.	3人1組になってください。	Make a group of three.
3.	2人でやってください。	Work in pairs.

↑ 両手の指をくっつけるしぐさ

4.	そのグループに入れてもらってね。	Join that group.
5.	他のグループと一緒になってください。	Join another group.
6.	もっと大きいグループを作りましょう。	Make a bigger group.
7.	大きな輪を作ってください。	Make a big circle.
8.	皆さん、由佳さんの後ろに並んでください。	Everyone, line up behind Yuka.
9.	列を作りましょう。	Form a line. / Form lines.
10.	2列に並んでください。	Make two lines.

11.	1列に並びましょう。	Stand in a line. / Get in a line.
12.	割り込みはいけませんよ。	Don't jump the line. / Don't cut into the line.

イ．カードを使って活動する Card Activity

1.	カードを（すべて）配ってください。	Deal (all) the cards.
2.	1人に4枚ずつ配ってください。	Deal four cards for each.
3.	カードがない人は手を挙げてね。	Raise your hand if you don't have one [a card].
4.	カードは裏返しにして［表を出して］ください。	Put your card(s) face down [face up].
5.	カードを机の上に広げましょう。	Spread the cards out on the desk.

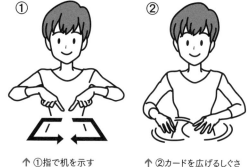

↑ ①指で机を示す　　↑ ②カードを広げるしぐさ

6.	自分のカードは見せないでね。	Don't show your cards to your friends.
7.	カードを戻してください。	Return the card(s) to the deck.
8.	ひと組のカードから1枚取ってください。	Pick a card from the deck.

9.	カードを切ってください。	Shuffle the cards.
10.	のぞいちゃいけませんよ。	Don't peek.
11.	このようにカードを持ってください。 ＊ジェスチャーをつけて	Hold the cards like this.
12.	カードが全部そろったら勝ち［上がり］ですよ。	You win when you complete your hand.
13.	ほしいカードをお願いしましょう。	Ask your friends for the card you want.

〈児童同士のカードのやりとり〉

14.	私にください…ありがとう。	Please give it to me.…Thank you.
	どういたしまして。	You're welcome.
15.	キングのカードを持っていますか？	Do you have a king card?
	はい、持っています。	Yes, I do.

ウ．カルタ・すごろくをする　Playing Japanese *Karuta* or *Sugoroku* Games

TRACK 01 08

1.	机を寄せてください。	Put your desks together.
2.	机をここに持ってきてください。	Move your desk over here.
3.	机を寄せて、大きなテーブルにしましょう。	Put your desks together to make a big table.
4.	全部片づけてください。	Put away everything. / Put everything away.
5.	絵カードを机に広げましょう。	Spread all the picture cards on the desk.

6.	文字カードは全部配ってください。	Deal out all the letter cards.
7.	あなたの番ですよ。	Your turn.
8.	1回休みです。	You lost your turn.
9.	上がりましたか？	Did you finish?

エ．ゲームをする Playing Games

((TRACK 01 09))

1.	ゲームをしましょう！	Let's play a game!
2.	最初はAグループです。 ＊Notes ②	Group A goes first.
3.	たくさんポイントを取ってくださいね。	Score as many as you can.
4.	1位には3点が入ります。	Three points for the first to finish.
5.	Bグループに1点入ります。	One point for Group B.
6.	日本語を使ったら減点ですよ。	You lose a point if you use Japanese.
7.	最初に5点を取ったチームが勝ちです。	The first team to get five points will win [wins].
8.	次は誰の番ですか？	Who goes next?
9.	一番点数が多いのは誰[どのチーム]ですか？	Who [Which team] got the most points?
10.	何点になりましたか？	What's your final score? / How many points?
11.	一緒に点数を数えましょう。	Let's count up the points together.
12.	あなた[Cグループ]の勝ちです。	You [Group C] won. / You're the winner. / Group C was the winner.

13. Ａグループがチャンピオンです。 Group A was the champion.

14. 引き分けですよ。 It's a tie [a draw].

↑ 線を引くように腕を伸ばす

15. おめでとう！ Congratulations!

Notes: ①勝敗にはこだわらないで

　子どもたちはゲームが大好き。楽しいゲームを通して、英語を用いるコミュニケーションへの積極的な態度や、集中して英語を聞く・話す力を無理なく養いたい。勝ち負けの要素が加わると「勝ちたい」欲求から活動への意欲が高まるように思われるが、勝敗にこだわるあまり日本語を多用したり、必要以上に競い合ったりすることは避ける。勝敗にはこだわらず、ゲームを上手に利用しよう。また、勝った児童やグループには、大きな拍手で頑張りをほめよう。

Notes: ②言葉の順序に気をつけて

　日本語の「Ａグループ」は、英語だと"Group A"、「Ａチーム」は"Team A"に。日本語と英語では、言葉の順序が逆になることもあるので気をつけよう。

作業・制作活動をするとき

Craft Activities

ア．紙を用いる活動をする Paper Craft

((• TRACK 01 10 •))

1. 鳥のところを切り抜いてください。 — Cut out a [the] bird.
2. のり付けしてください。 — Paste it. / Glue it.
3. 2つ折りにしましょう。 — Fold it in half.
4. 折り紙を山折りにしてください。 — Fold the sheet with the colored side out.
5. 赤く塗りましょう。 — Color it red.
6. 赤で線をなぞってください。 — Trace the line in red.
7. 三角に折ってください。 — Fold the paper into a triangle.
8. 紙を半分に切ってください。 — Cut the paper in half.
9. ごみは落ちていませんか？ 拾ってください。 — No trash around you? Pick it up.
10. それはゴミ箱に入れてね。 — Put it [them] in the trash can.

イ．道具を使う Using Tools

((• TRACK 01 11 •))

1. はさみを使います。 — You'll need some scissors.
2. クレヨンを出してください。 — Take out your crayons.
3. コンパスをケースにしまいましょう。 — Put your compass back into your case.

4. 消しゴムを自動車に見立てますよ。　(Imagine) your eraser is a car.

5. 何か足りませんか？　What (else) do you need?

6. のり[はさみ]がなかったら手を挙げてください。　Raise your hand if you don't have glue [scissors, etc.].

7. マジックペンを（こちらによこして）ください。　Pass the marker to me.

8. 全部片づけましょう。　Put everything away.

9. 机の上を片づけてください。　Clear up your desk.

10. 定規は机にしまってください。　Put your ruler into your desk.

11. 友だちと一緒に使いましょう。　You have to share it [them].

12. ナイフには気をつけてください。　Be careful with your knife.

ウ．絵・図を描く　Drawing Pictures or Figures

TRACK 01 12

1. このように線を引いてください。　Draw a line this way.

2. 縦[横]に線を引きましょう。　Draw a vertical [horizontal] line.

3. 線をまっすぐに引いてください。　Draw a straight line.

4. 点線[波線]を引いてください。　Draw a dotted [wavy] line.

5. 右上[左下]に名前を書きましょう。　Write your name at [in] the upper right [lower left] corner.

6. 画面の下［中央］に川を描いてください。	Draw a river at the bottom [in the center] of the picture.
7. 茂みにウサギを３匹描き入れてください。	Put [Draw] three rabbits in the bushes.
8. 唇は赤く塗りましょう。	Color the lips red.
9. 海の魚を○で囲んでください。	Circle the fish in the sea.
10. 魚が描けていなかったら１点減点です。	Minus one point for no fish.

Notes: 英語で頭と身体を動かそう

　英語の指示で作業・制作活動を行い、頭と身体を同時に動かすことで学習効率が高まる。発話の負担がない点では、英語学習の初心者に適した活動といえる。英語で指示を出す際は、ジェスチャーをふんだんに用いて、理解を促すようにしよう。「図を描く」p.124 も参照。

Chapter 5 演じる活動をするとき
Acting

1.	お医者さんのつもりになってください。	You're a doctor. / Play the role of doctor.
2.	映画館にいるつもりになってください。	Imagine you're in a movie theater.
3.	山田先生のつもりになってください。	Do like Mr. Yamada.
4.	看護師さんになりたい人はいますか？	Who wants to be a nurse?
5.	あなたは銀行員です。	You will be a bank clerk.
6.	この会話を演技でやってみましょう。	Let's act out this conversation, shall we?
7.	あなたはお母さん役ですよ。	You play the role of the mother.
8.	あなたから会話を始めてください。	You start the dialog.
9.	メモを見ないで言ってください。	Now try without notes.
10.	もらったら「ありがとう」と言いましょう。	Say "thank you" when you get them.
11.	「どういたしまして」を忘れないようにしてくださいね。	Don't forget (to say) "You're welcome."
12.	背景を黒板に描いてください。	Draw some scenery on the board.
13.	他にやりたい人はいますか？	Anybody else wants to try?

Chapter 6 クイズ・歌の活動をするとき

Quiz and Singing Time

ア．クイズの活動をする　Quiz Time　🔊 TRACK 01 14

1.	クイズを出しますよ。	Here's a riddle [a quiz].
2.	クイズを出してください。	Give us your riddle.
3.	簡単なクイズです。	It's a simple riddle.
4.	ヒントをあげますね。	I'll give you some hints.
5.	3番目のヒントです。	This is the third hint.
6.	5番目のヒントでもわからなかったら負けですよ。	You'll lose if you can't find the answer at the fifth hint.
7.	わかった人は手を挙げてください。	Raise your hand when [if] you know the answer.
8.	友達に教えてはいけません。	Don't tell your friends about the answer.
9.	もっと時間が欲しいですか？	Do you need more time?
10.	まだわかりませんか？	You still haven't got it?

イ．歌う活動をする　Singing Songs　🔊 TRACK 01 15

1.	歌いましょう。	Let's sing a song, shall we?
2.	歌いたいですか？	Do you want to sing?
3.	まず、曲を聴きましょう。	Let's listen to the melody first.
4.	この歌を聞いたことのある人はいますか？	Who has heard this song before?

5.	その曲を聞いたことがあるでしょう。	You know the melody, don't you?
6.	歌詞を説明しますね。	I'll explain the words first.
7.	誰が歌っているでしょうか?	Who's the singer? / Do you know the singer?
8.	CDに合わせて歌いましょう。	Sing along with the CD.
9.	直人、一緒に歌ってください。	Join in singing, Naoto.
10.	私のギターに合わせて歌ってください。	Please sing along with my guitar.
11.	これは「大きな古時計」の替え歌ですね?	This song has the same melody as *My Grandfather's Clock*, doesn't it?
12.	もっと大きな声で歌いましょう。	Let's sing louder, please.

Chapter 7

DVD・ビデオや絵本・紙芝居などを観るとき
DVD /Video or Story /Japanese Kamishibai Time

TRACK 01 16

1.	さあ、お話[紙芝居]が始まりますよ。	Now it's story [*Kamishibai*] time.
2.	テレビ[紙芝居]の前に集まってください。	Go and sit before [in front of] the television [*Kamishibai* /storyteller with pictures].
3.	面白い番組[お話]ですよ。	Here's an interesting program [story].
4.	皆さん、見えますか？	Can everybody see?
5.	よく見ていてくださいね。	Watch it carefully.
6.	物語の長さはほんの2分です。	It's only two minutes long.
7.	だいたいわかりましたか？	Did you get the main idea?
8.	お話には誰が出てきたでしょうか？	Who are the people in the story?
9.	どんな動物[フルーツ]が出てきましたか？	What animal(s) [fruit(s)] did you see?
10.	どのような話でしたか？	What's the story about?
11.	ネコは何と言っていましたか？	What did the cat say?
12.	何匹のサルが[何個のリンゴが]出てきましたか？	How many monkeys [apples] did you see?

Chapter 8 ストーリー・テリング
Storytelling

① 絵本の読み聞かせ法 How to tell stories

絵本には、その目的に応じて色々な読み聞かせの方法がある。ここでは英語を児童に理解しやすいよう読み聞かせ、また読み手にたくさん英語を発話させながらやり取りする方法を紹介しよう。

a 絵本を開く前に　　　　　　　　　Before opening the book

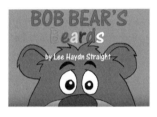

読み聞かせの前に、表紙を示しながら絵やタイトルから内容を類推させ、これから始まる物語や登場するキャラクターへの興味を喚起しよう。絵を示しながら、児童が既習の英語で答えられそうな簡単な質問を投げかけてやり取りしたり、タイトルを一緒に読むことを促したりする。この時点ではまだ答えられない質問を投げかけ、答えを読み聞かせのあとに考えてみよう、などとストーリーへの期待をふくらませてもよい。

TRACK 01 17

1.	今日はどんな本を持って来たでしょう？	Guess what story book I have today?
2.	これは何ですか？	What's this?
3.	この動物の名前を知っていますか？	Do you know the name of this animal?
4.	そうですね。これはクマですね。	That's right. It's a bear.
5.	これは何色ですか？	What color is this?
6.	茶色かな？それとも黒色ですか？	Is it brown or black?

7.	本のタイトルは何でしょう？	What's the title of this book?
8.	ここです。読めますか？	Here. Can you read it?
9.	先生が読むので一緒に読みましょう。	I am going to read it. Can you read along?
10.	準備はいいですか？いち、に…	Are you ready? One, two…
11.	beards の意味はわかりますか。	What does "beards" mean?
12.	さあ、なんでしょうね。	We'll see.　＊すぐ答えを出さないで児童に考えさせたい時
13.	あとでわかるようになりますよ。	We will find it out.

b 読み聞かせ　　Storytelling

　読み聞かせは、聞き手の様子をしっかり観察しながら行おう。また、内容によってはリズムや抑揚・強弱をつけ、時には間を取りながら感情を込めて読むようにする。同じセンテンスが何度も繰り返される時には、ジェスチャーやキューを出して一緒に読むように誘うのもよいだろう。ストーリー展開への興味を持たせながら、お話の世界へ引き込むように質問を投げかけよう。原因と結果が繰り返されるお話の場合には、ページをめくる前に次の展開をみんなで予想しながら発話を促すのもよい。

本文①　　((TRACK 01 18))

On Monday, Bob Bear ate some juicy strawberries, and got...

Chapter 8 | ストーリー・テリング

（ページをめくる）

…a RED beard!

1. わあ、見てごらん。
   ＊クマの口のまわりを指しながら

   Wow! Look at this.

2. 何色ですか？

   What color is this?

   （生徒：赤です。）

   (Student: Red.)

本文②

(((• TRACK 01 19 •)))

On Tuesday, Bob Bear ate some sweet carrot soup, and got…

1. 何曜日ですか？

   What day is it?

   （生徒：火曜日です。）

   (Students: Tuesday.)

2. 何を食べましたか？

   What did he eat?

   （生徒：甘いニンジンのスープです。）

   (Students: Some sweet carrot soup.)

3. 何が起こるでしょうか？

   What's going to happen? / What do you think is going to happen?

本文③

（ページをめくる）

(((• TRACK 01 20 •)))

…an ORANGE beard!

1. 当たっていましたね。	You are right. / You guessed it right.
2. すばらしい！	Great! / Good job!

C 読後活動　　　　　　　　　　After storytelling

　読み聞かせのあとは、お話を振り返る時間を持つことで内容が理解できたか確認するとともに、児童の発話の機会を作るようにしたい。絵本の流れを示す絵カードなどがあれば、それを並べかえながら登場人物の名前を思い出したり、そのせりふを言ってみたりすることもできる。また、読み聞かせは1度で終わらせず、2度目は文字を指さしながら教師と交互に読む、あるいはせりふの部分は児童に読ませるといった読みのバリエーションも広げよう。

　絵本をほぼ読めるようになった場合は、それを読み手として発表させたり、その絵本のフォーマットをもとにオリジナルな物語を考えるといった発展活動もできる。

TRACK 01 21

1. 覚えていますか？　ボブベアが苺を食べた時、口の周りにできたのは？	Do you remember? When Bob Bear ate strawberries, he got … what?
2. 今度は一緒に読んでみましょうか。	Can we read the story together this time?
3. 新しいお話を考えましょう。ボブベアが何を食べたら？　何色のひげができましたか？	Let's make a new story. When Bob Bear ate… what? What color did his beard become?

Notes: 絵本 *Bob Bear's beards* by Lee Haydn Straight (https://www.youtube.com/watch?v=HqMkJx1u4iM)

Chapter 8 | ストーリー・テリング

② ストーリー・テリング Storytelling

a お話 — Stories

((• TRACK 01 22 •))

1. お話は楽しく面白い。
   Stories can be fun and interesting.

2. 物語から児童は異文化を知ることができる。
   Children can learn about other cultures from stories. / Stories can introduce children to other cultures.

3. 子どもはお話を通して実生活を違う視点から見ることができる。
   Children can look at real life from different viewpoints through stories.

4. 子どもはお話を聞いて正しい読み方を身につけることができる。
   Children can acquire good intonation by listening to stories.

b お話タイム — Story time

((• TRACK 01 23 •))

1. さあ、お話の時間ですよ。ここに［私の周りに］座って。
   OK, everybody. It's story time. Come and sit around here [around me].

2. さあ、英語のお話タイムですよ。
   Listen, it's time for English storytelling.

3. スクリーンを見てください。先生が何のお話をするのか当ててみよう。
   Please look at the screen, and guess what story I'm going to tell you.

4. 始めに先生の話を［CDを］聞いて、話のタイトルをみんなで言ってみよう。
   First, listen to me [to the CD], and say the title of the story together.

I 小学校英語

c お話の仕方 — How to tell stories

((• TRACK 01 24 •))

1. これから桃太郎の話をします。 — I'm going to tell you a story about *Peach Boy*...
2. 話に出てくる単語を全部知らなくてもいいですよ。 — You don't have to know every word in the story.
3. でも、話のすじは理解できたほうがいいね。 — But you should understand the storyline.
4. お話をする時は、自然な調子で。 — When you tell a story, speak naturally.

d お話のための質問 — Story questions

((• TRACK 01 25 •))

1. お話でピーナッツを欲しがったのは誰？ — Who wanted peanuts in the story?
2. キツネは旅人に何と言いましたか。 — What did the fox say to the travel(l)er?
3. サルは最初どんな気持ちでしたか。 — How did the monkey feel at first?
4. その鳥はなぜ幸せに感じたのでしょう。 — Why did the bird feel happy?

e 確認用質問 — Confirmation questions

((• TRACK 01 26 •))

1. 太郎は何回 Thank you. と言いましたか。 — How many times did Taro say "Thank you."?

2. reading cards を取り出して、お話の順序に並べなさい。	Take out your reading cards, and arrange them in the right order. ＊reading cards＝Notes参照
3. お話の斜体語［下線を引いた語］を別の表現で置き換えるとどうなりますか。	How can you rephrase the italicized [underlined] words in the story?
4. そのお話に関してどう思った？	Tell me what you think about the story.

Notes: reading cards は話の筋を絵にした複数のカード。内容をどの程度理解し、把握しているかを振り返るために並べさせる。

f 話題 — Topics of stories

TRACK 01 27

1. この物語の主題は何ですか。	What is the topic of this story?
2. この物語の主人公（たち）をどう思いますか。	What do you think of [about] the main character(s) in this story?
3. 日本の物語と比べて似ている点はどこでしょうか。また違っている点は？	What points are similar to Japanese stories? Or, what points are different from them?
4. この物語は好きですか？ その理由は何ですか？	Do you like this story? And please tell me why.

g 読みに誘う　　Inviting Students to Tell [Read] Stories

1. さあ一緒に読んでみましょう。いいですか？	Let's read aloud together. Ready?
2. この犬のせりふはみんなで読みます。いいですか？	Read this line from the dog in chorus. OK?
3. これは何？　この子は何をやっているの？　＊絵を指しながら	What's this? What is he doing?
4. 絵本の 10 ページにいすはいくつありますか。	On page 10 of your picture book, how many chairs do you see?
5. 5 ページの絵を見てごらん。マイクは手にマジックペンを持っています。何色かな？	Look at the picture on page 5. Mike has a marker pen [Magic Marker] in his hand. What color is it [this pen]?
6. 彼は何をしようとしているのかな？	What is he going to do next?
7. 誰かわかる人？　手を挙げて。	Who can tell me? Raise your hands.

Classroom English Handbook

一般的指示

General Directions

Chapter 1 移　動
Movement

a 席の移動 — Changing seats

TRACK 02 01

1.	座りなさい。	Sit down.
2.	早く座って。	Take your seats quickly.
3.	席に戻りなさい。	Go (back) to your seat.
4.	立ち上がって動き回りなさい。	Stand up and move around.
5.	自由に動き回ってもいいですよ。	You are free to move around.
6.	質問に答えられる人を見つけなさい。	Find someone who can answer the questions.
7.	隣の人と対面しなさい。	Stand face to face with your neighbor [partner].
8.	聞きたいことを誰に聞いてもいいよ。	You may ask anyone, anything you like.
9.	よし、班ごとに作業。	OK, let's make [get into] groups.
10.	好きなように3人の班になって。	Get into groups of three as you like.

生徒の応答 Student Response

席を離れていい？	Can we leave our seats now?
今日の席はいつもと同じ？	Is today's seating as usual?
席替えしてほしい。	We want a new seating order.

b 教室内（から）の移動　　Moving in and out of the classroom

TRACK 02 02

1. 黒板の所に行って。	Will you go up to the board?
2. 黒板の所に来て。	Come up to the blackboard.
3. OHP（スクリーン）のそばに来て。	Come and stand by the overhead projector (screen).
4. こちらに来るのは誰の番ですか？	Whose turn is it to come over here?
5. コンピュータ［マルチメディア］活用室へ行きましょう。	Let's go to the CALL [multimedia] room.　＊CALL＝Computer Assisted Language Learning
6. 視聴覚室に行ってビデオを見ようか。	How about going to the AV room and watching a video?　＊AV＝Audio-Visual
7. では退出していいです。	You can go out now. / OK, you can leave. / You may leave the room now.
8. 今日はこれで終わり。退出。	That's all for today. You are free to go.
9. OK、各自解散。	OK. Please find your way out.

教師と生徒のやりとり Interaction

S: 教室を出てもいいですか？	Can I go out of the classroom?
T: どうしたの？	Why?
S: ロッカーに辞書を置いてきました。	I left my dictionary in my locker.
T: なるほど。ほかに忘れた人は？　取りに行ってきていいよ。急いで！	I see. Anyone else? OK. You can go and get it. But hurry back.

Chapter 2 注 目

Directing Students' Attention

a 板書に — To the blackboard

TRACK 02 03

1. こっちを向いて。これから話すことは大事な点だ。 — Look (here)! This is important.
2. 弘、これ見える？ — Hiroshi, can you see this?
3. 美香、これを読んで。 — Mika, read this, please.
4. これを見て、注意して聞いてください。 — Look at this and listen carefully, please.
5. みんな、注意して。 — Attention, everyone(, please).
6. この文を見て私に続いて繰り返しましょう。 — Look at this sentence and repeat after me.

b 生徒に — To the students

TRACK 02 04

1. 直美に注目。 — Look at Naomi.
2. 彼女の口（の動き）を見て。 — Watch her mouth.
3. 隣の人と向き合って。 — Face your partner [neighbor].
4. 正人が何を用意しているか見てみよう。 — Let's see what Masato has to [will] show us.
5. 令子がその文の意味を身振りで表すのを見てみよう。 — We'll see how Reiko acts out the sentence.

6.	久美の手の動きを注意深く見て。	Watch the movement of Kumi's hands carefully.
7.	私の話を聞きながら克彦を見ていてください。	Listen to me and keep your eyes on Katsuhiko.

c 教師に / To the teacher

1.	注目！	Look! / Here! / Look here. / Look at me.
2.	私［先生］をまっすぐ見て。	Look directly at me.
3.	私の口元をよく見て。	Look at my mouth closely [carefully].
4.	私の身振りを見て。何をしているでしょう。	Look at my gestures. Guess what I am doing.
5.	私が指さしている物は何でしょう。	Tell me what I am pointing at.
6.	私から目をそらさないで。	Don't turn your eyes away. / Don't look away from me.
7.	よく注意して見て。	Give me all your attention.

d 参観者に / To the observer(s)

1.	ご覧のように、本日は多くのお客様がおいでです。	As you can see, we have lots of guests today.
2.	こちらが本日のお客さまです。	Here is our guest today.

3.	こちらがアメリカ（合衆国）からいらしたキャロル・グリーンさんです。	This is Ms. Carol Green from the United States.
4.	本日はこの市の多くの先生方が皆さんの授業を見においでです。	Many teachers in this city have come to see you today.
5.	後ろを向いてお客様に「おはようございます」と言いなさい。	Turn around and say, "Good morning" to them.
6.	本日は皆さんのご両親もお見えです。	Some of your parents are with us today.

Notes: 2は客が一人の場合。3はformal. 姓もつけて紹介する。4は研究授業。6は父母の授業参観日などに。

e 図・絵に — To the picture(s)

(TRACK 02 07)

1.	ご覧なさい。	Look! / There!
2.	スクリーンをご覧なさい。	Look at the screen.
3.	53ページの絵をご覧なさい。	Look at the pictures on page 53.
4.	絵を見ながらCDを聞きましょう。	Look at the pictures and listen to the CD, will you?
5.	振り向いて後ろの地図を見てください。	Turn around and look at the map at the back of the room.
6.	53ページの写真に写っているマイクのいとこを見つけたかな？	Can you see Mike's cousins in the picture on page 53?

Chapter 2 | 注目

7. 暗くて見えない。明かりをつけてください。	It's too dark. Will you turn [switch / put] on the light?

Notes: 7 はその日の天候等によって。

f 窓の外に — Outside the classroom

TRACK 02 08

1. 外を見てみよう。	Look out of the window. / Let's look outside.
2. 庭に面白いものがありますよ。	There's something interesting in the garden.
3. 葉がしだいに黄色になってきていますね。	The leaves are getting more and more yellow, aren't they?
4. 向こうの赤い花が見えるかい。今、満開だ。	Can you see those red flowers over there? They're in full bloom.
5. 英語ではあの花を何というのかな。＊4に続けて	What do you call those flowers in English?

教師と生徒のやりとり Interaction

T: どのページかわかっていますか。	What page are you on?
S: ここですか。	Is this the page?
T: 違います。55ページです。	No. You must turn to page 55.
S: あっ、そうだ。すみません。	Oh, I see. I'm sorry.

Chapter 3 起立・着席

Standing Up and Sitting Down

a 起 立 — Standing up

ア．個人で Individual(s)   (TRACK 02 09)

1.	立って。	Stand up.
2.	立ってもらいたい。	I want you to stand up. / I'd like you to stand up.
3.	立ってくれますか。	Will [Can] you stand up? / Would [Could] you stand up?
4.	花梨さん、立ってください。	Please stand up, Karin.
5.	立って［起きて］ください。	Please get up.
6.	お立ち願えませんか。	Would you mind standing up?

Notes: would [could] you 〜？を使ったほうが丁寧。

イ．列・班ごとに In row(s) or group(s)   (TRACK 02 10)

1.	この列、立ってください。	This row, stand up.
2.	この班、立ってください。	This group, please stand up together.
3.	後ろの列の人だけ立ってください。	I'd like only the back row of students to stand up.
4.	左側の列の人、立ってくれますか。	The students on the left, will [can] you stand up?

5.	A班、教壇の上に立ってくれますか。	Group A, would [could] you stand on the platform?
6.	次の班、急いで立って。	Next group, get up quick!
7.	男子だけ立ってくれませんか。	Only boys, would you mind standing up?

ウ．ペアで In pair(s) 〔TRACK 02 11〕

1.	君たち2人、立ってください。	Stand up. You, two. / Please stand up, both of you. / I want you to stand in pairs.
2.	今度はこの2人の番です。立ってください。	This pair's turn. Please get up.
3.	起立して向かい合ってください。	I'd like you to stand face to face.
4.	君たち2人、黒板の前に立ってくれる？	Will you two stand in front of the blackboard?
5.	優子と美紀、立ってこの対話文を読んでごらん。	Yuko and Miki, would you stand up and read this dialog?
6.	隣の人と立ってくれますか。	Would you mind standing with your partner?

エ．全員で In the whole class 〔TRACK 02 12〕

1.	全員起立。	Everybody, stand up. / All rise. / I want all of you to stand up. / Would you please all stand up?
2.	全員、列ごとに立ってください。	I'd like you all to stand in rows.
3.	全員立って歌いましょう。	Let's all stand up and sing a song!

生徒の応答 Student Response

また僕？	Me again?
この前もやりました。	I did it last time.
ちょっと待って。	Give me [us] more time.

b 着席 — Sitting down

ア．個人で Individual(s)   (TRACK 02 13)

1. 座って。
   Sit down. / Sit in [on] your seat. / You may [can] sit at your desk. / Have a seat. / Take your seat.

2. 弘、座ってください。
   Please sit down, Hiroshi.

イ．複数人で In group(s)   (TRACK 02 14)

1. （複数の人に）座って。
   Sit in [on] your seats. / You may [can] sit at your desks. / Take your seats. / Have a seat.

2. ２人とも座って（ください）。
   Please sit down, you two. / Sit in your seats. / Have a seat, both of you.

3. この班は座ってください。
   This group, please sit down.

4. いいでしょう。席に戻ってください。
   OK. (Go) back [Return] to your seats.

5. 全員、着席。
   Everybody, sit down. / Take your seats, all of you.

Notes: have a seat は相手が複数でも a seat.

Chapter 4 注意・叱責
Warning / Scolding

ⓐ 静かに — Be quiet

ア．クラス全体に To the class
((• TRACK 02 15 •))

1. 静粛に。
   Sshh! / Quiet! / Hush! / Silence! / Button your lips.
2. 静かにしてください。
   Quiet, please. / Please quiet down. / Please be quiet. / Be silent, everyone. / Be quiet, will you? / Will you be quiet?

Notes: 一般に注意・叱責は表現そのものよりもイントネーション、声の強さ、高さ、響き、また表情やジェスチャーによってその程度が違ってくることを考慮したい。

イ．個々の生徒に To individuals
((• TRACK 02 16 •))

1. 俊子、うるさいな。静かにして。
   Toshiko! You're too noisy. I need [want] you to be quiet.
2. 誰だ、うるさくしているのは。
   Who is making this noise?
3. 山田、口を閉じて。
   Yamada, close your mouth.
4. 賢二、あまりうるさくするな。和子の話が聞こえない。
   Kenji, don't make such a [so much] noise. I can't hear Kazuko.

生徒の応答 Student Response

すみません。	Sorry. / I'm sorry.
私じゃありません。	Not me. / It's not me.

b 顔を上げて — Looking up

((• TRACK 02 17 •))

1. 顔を上げて。
   Look up! / Faces up! / Face forward! / Face the front!

2. 顔を上げて先生［黒板］に注目。
   Look (up) at me [at the (black)board].

3. 下を見ないで顔を上げなさい。
   Don't look down. Look up.

c 私語の禁止 — No whispering

ア．最初の注意 First admonishing

((• TRACK 02 18 •))

1. 私語はやめろ。
   No talking! / No whispering! / Don't talk! / Don't whisper!

2. 何を話してる。やめなさい。
   What are you talking about? Stop it!

3. 授業中の私語は駄目！
   No whispering is allowed in class!

4. 話すのをやめて聞きなさい。
   Don't talk, but listen. / Stop talking and listen to me.

5. 私が話しています。
   I am talking now.　　＊I amに強いアクセントを置く

イ．（注意してもやめないので）しかる Scolding

((• TRACK 02 19 •))

1. また騒々しくなったな。
   It's getting noisy again.

2. 隣席の人とおしゃべりするなと言ったでしょう。
   I told you not to talk with your neighbor.

3. まだおしゃべりしている。今すぐやめなさい。
   You're still talking. Stop it right now.

Chapter 4 | 注意・叱責

d いたずらの禁止　　No mischief

ア．短い注意　Shorter warning　　TRACK 02 20

1. 静かに座っていて。　　Sit still.
2. 今すぐそれをやめて。　　Stop it right now!
3. 二度とやるなよ。　　Never do that again!
4. 何をやっているの。　　What are you doing?
   ＊とがめる調子で

イ．長めの注意　Longer warning　　TRACK 02 21

1. やめなさい。二度とやらないで。　　Stop it and (be sure you) don't do it again.
2. 君たちのやっているのはいけないことでしょう。すぐやめなさい。　　You're doing what you shouldn't. Stop it right now.

e その他の注意　　Others

TRACK 02 22

1. 正面を向いて。　　Turn around and face the front.
   ＊後部座席の生徒に話しかけている生徒に
2. 机をまっすぐにして。　　Straighten your desk(s).
3. 辞書はしまって。　　Put away your dictionaries.
4. 教科書はどこまで進んでいる？　45ページだ。　　Find where we are in the textbook. We are on page 45.
5. 教科書以外は全部片付けて。　　Clear your desks of everything but your textbook.
6. 机の上に全部出しなさい。時間を無駄にするな。　　Get everything ready on your desk. Don't waste any time!

Ⅱ 一般的指示

45

Chapter 5 発言

Remarks / Responses

a 大きな声で（言う・話す） — Louder

TRACK 02 23

1. もっと大きな声で言ってください。	Louder! / A bit louder. / You can speak louder, can't you?
2. 大きな声でお願いします。	In a big voice, please. / Please speak up. / Could you speak in a louder voice, please?
3. 皆に聞こえるように大きな声で。	Speak up so that everyone can hear you.

b もっとはっきりと — Clearer

TRACK 02 24

1. はっきりと（言ってください）。	Clearly, please.
2. もっとはっきりと言ってください。	Speak more clearly. / Could you say it more clearly?
3. 大きくはっきりと言ってください。	Could you speak loud and clear, please?
4. 一語一語もっとはっきりと。	Say each word more clearly.
5. 単語をもっとはっきりと発音するように。	Try to pronounce your words more clearly.

生徒の応答 Student Response

風邪で声が出ません。	I can't speak (any) louder because I have a cold.
この単語の発音がわかりません。	I don't know how to pronounce this word.

c 口を大きく開けて　　　With the mouth wide-open

((• TRACK 02 25 •))

1. 口を大きく開けて。　　Open your mouth wide.

2. 口を大きく開けて話してみなさい。　　Try to speak with your mouth wide open.

3. 音読する時は恥ずかしがらず口を大きく開けなさい。　　Don't hesitate to open your mouth wide when you read aloud.

4. 音読する時は口が十分開いているかを確認しなさい。　　Always check that your mouth is wide open when you read aloud.

Notes: 4 は発音指導の際の注意。

d 意味を考えて　　　With meaning in mind

((• TRACK 02 26 •))

1. 意味を考えなさい。　　Think about the meaning. / Try to keep the meaning in (your) mind.

2. 意味にもっと注意して。　　Pay more attention to the meaning.

3. 読解においては、いつも話の筋を忘れないように。　　Always try to remember the story when reading [you read]. / Don't lose the story line when reading.

4. このシーンで主人公がどんな気持ちでいたかを考えなさい。　　Think about how the hero [the heroine] feels in this scene.

5. もし主人公の立場だったらと考えてください。　　Suppose (that) you are in the hero's [heroine's] position.

Notes: 本文の読解を終えた音読練習の段階での指示。

e 発言を促す　　Stimulating students to talk

ア．答えを促す　Encouraging students to answer　(TRACK 02 27)

1. （答えの）準備ができたかな。
   Ready? / Be ready with your answer. / Are you ready to answer?

2. 私の質問に答えてもらおう。
   I want you to answer my questions.

3. 私の質問に単純に「はい」か「いいえ」で答えなさい。
   Answer my questions simply with "yes" or "no".

4. 推測して［やって］ごらん。
   Why don't you make a guess [try]?

5. 考えていることを皆に発表してごらん。
   Will you tell us what you think?

イ．質問を受ける　Eliciting questions　(TRACK 02 28)

1. 何か質問は？
   Any questions? / Do you have any questions? / Are there any questions?

2. もう質問はないですか。
   No further questions? / No more questions? / Is everything clear now? / Any other questions?

3. 今日の授業はわかったかな。
   Do you understand today's lesson?

4. 質問があったら何でも自由に聞いて。
   Feel free to ask whatever questions you have.

f 挙手　　Raising one's hand

((• TRACK 02 29 •))

1. 手を挙げて。	Hands up. / Put your hand up. / Raise your hand.
2. この質問に答えられる人は挙手。	Who knows the answer to this question? Hands up. / Put your hand up if you know the answer to this question.
3. この質問に答えてみようと思う人は？	(Are there) any volunteers for this question?
4. 質問があったら手を挙げて、私の話を中断してよい。	If there are any questions, just put your hand up and stop me.
5. 誰が挙手しているか見えない。手をまっすぐ挙げて。	I can't see whose hands are up. Put your hands up straight.
6. 挙手を数えている間、手を下ろさないで。	Keep your hands up while I count them.

教師と生徒のやりとり Interaction

T: 本文について何か質問があったら手を挙げてください。	If you have any questions about the text, put your hand up, please.
S: （挙手し）質問があります。	I have a question.
T: 鈴木君、どこがわからないの？	Yes, Suzuki-kun, what is your problem?
S: 5行目のitが何を指すかわかりません.	I don't know the meaning of 'it' on line 5.
T: itは前の行のthe customを意味します。	This 'it' stands for 'the custom' found in the previous line.
S: わかりました。	Oh, now I see.

Chapter 6 ほめる
Praising

a 一般的なほめ言葉 — Praise in general

(((• TRACK 02 30 •)))

1. いいね。 — Good. → Great. → Splendid. → Excellent. → Fantastic. / Marvelous. / Terrific. / Magnificent.
2. よろしい［正解］。 — Right. / Fine. / Yes. / That's correct. / Just right.
3. すばらしい。 — Beautiful. / Impressive. / Wonderful. / Super. / Superb.
4. 完ぺきです。 — Perfect. / Flawless.
5. 大変結構です。 — Very good.
6. そのほうがいいです。 — That's better.
7. それが私の欲しかった答えです。 — That's what I've wanted.
8. 理想的な答えです。 — A very good job. / An ideal answer.

Notes: 1 は後半ほどほめ方の程度が上がる（/ で並列したものは同程度）。3 の super, superb はラテン語の super-（〜の上、〜を超えて）の意味から。

b 声の質 — Voice quality

(((• TRACK 02 31 •)))

1. あなたの声はよく通る。 — Your voice carries well.
2. はっきりした声ですね。 — You have a clear voice. / You speak very clearly.

Chapter 6 | ほめる

3. 穏やかで素敵な声ですね。	What a nice soft voice you have!
4. いい声ですね。	Your voice is nice [very good]. / You have a really good voice.
5. 大きくはっきりした声ですね。	You read in a loud, clear voice.
6. ありがとう。素敵で明快な声でした。	Thank you. That was nice and clear.

c 声の大きさ — Loudness of voice

TRACK 02 32

1. 大きな声で読んでくれてありがとう。	Thanks for reading in a loud voice.
2. 今度は聞こえます。	Now I can hear you.
3. はい。その位の大きさで十分。	Good. That's loud enough.
4. 大変結構です。声も声の大きさもいいですね。	Pretty good. That's nice and loud.

d 努力 — Students' effort

ア．成果に対して To the result of the effort

TRACK 02 33

1. よくできました。	A good job. / Nice work. / Well done. / Good for you!
2. すごくいい出来じゃないの！	Isn't that a great job?
3. 大変よくできました。	What beautiful work! / You did a wonderful job. / You've done that very nicely.

| 4. 今度は本当によくできました。 | You did really well this time. |

イ．ねぎらう Appreciating the students' effort

((TRACK 02 34))

1. 試してくれてありがとう。	Thank you for trying.
2. いつもよく頑張るね。	You always work hard. / You always try your best. / You always put effort into your work. / You're such a hard worker.
3. 一生懸命取り組んだのですね。	You must have worked hard on this. / You have really been studying hard, haven't you?

e 手書きの文字 — Hand writing

((TRACK 02 35))

| 1. よく書けているね。 | Very good. / Neat writing. / You write very clearly [legibly]. |
| 2. あなたの字はきれいですね。 | Your handwriting is neat. / You have beautiful handwriting. / You write beautifully [very well]. |

f 向上の度合い — Improvement

((TRACK 02 36))

1. ずっと良くなっています。	You're much better. / You're getting better. / What an improvement! / You've improved a lot [so much].
2. 今度はずっと良くできましたね。	You did much better this time, didn't you?
3. あなたが進歩したのでうれしいです。	I'm pleased with your improvement. / A great improvement! That makes me very happy.

g 試験の結果 — Results of the test

1. 満点。 — Full marks. / Perfect answer. / You got a hundred percent. / You got a perfect score. / Your answer is just perfect.
2. おめでとう。よくできました。 — Congratulations! You did a good job.
3. この試験で9割できています。 — You got 90 percent on this exam.
4. 満点に近いです。 — You were close to the top score.
5. このクラスが一番よくできました。 — Your class has done the best of all.
6. いい出来だけどまだ少しもの足りないな。 — That's good, but you're still missing some points.

生徒の応答 Student Response

英語の試験は満点だ。	I got the top score on the English exam.
英語はAでした。	I got an A in English.
まあまあでした。	So-so. / Not bad.
結果にがっかりしている。	I'm disappointed with the result.
次回頑張るよ。	I'll do better next time.

Chapter 7 励まし
Encouragement

a 希望をもたせる — Hope

(((• TRACK 02 38 •)))

1. あきらめるな。 — Don't give up.
2. 次回はもっと良くできるよ。 — You'll do better next time. / I know you will do better next time.
3. 次回は試験に合格するよ。 — I'm sure you will pass the test next time.
4. もう一回やってごらん。今度はきっと良くなっていると思う。 — Try it again. I'm sure you can do better this time.
5. 正しくやれるようになるまで続けてごらん。 — Keep trying until you get it right.
6. 次回は万事うまくいくだろう。 — Everything will be OK next time.
7. 心配するな。まだやれるよ。 — Don't worry. You can still do it.

b 意欲をかき立てる — Motivating

(((• TRACK 02 39 •)))

1. 元気を出して。 — Cheer up.
2. 気を楽に。 — Take it easy.
3. あきらめないで頑張れ。 — Stick it out. / Stick to it.
4. 幸運を祈る。 — I wish you good luck [the best].

Chapter 7 | 励まし

c 積極性を引き出す — Positive attitude

TRACK 02 40

1. 元気を出して言ってみて。 — Speak up.
2. 元気を出して。 — Come on.
3. 引っ込み思案にならないで。 — Don't be shy.
4. 思いきってやってみろ。 — Give it a try [a go].
5. やってみる価値があるよ。 — It's worth a try.
6. 思いきって自分の考え［意見］を言ってみなさい。 — Feel free to say what you think. / Feel free to give your opinion.
7. 間違うことを恐れないで。 — Don't be afraid of making mistakes.

d 好調を持続させる — Keeping students in (good) condition

TRACK 02 41

1. その調子だ。 — That's it. / That's the spirit. / You're doing fine.
2. その調子で続けなさい。 — Keep working. / Don't slow down. / Stick to your work.
3. その調子で頑張りなさい。 — Keep up the good work.
4. そのやり方でいいよ。 — You're on the right track.
5. 万事うまくいっているんだね。 — Everything is all right, isn't it?

e 慰め・同情 — Sympathy

TRACK 02 42

1. ついてなかったね。 — Bad luck!
2. それは残念ですね。 — What a shame [pity]! / That's a shame [pity]. / Isn't that a shame [pity]?
3. それは大変ですね。 — That's terrible [awful / too bad]. / How terrible [awful]!
4. 心配するな。 — Never mind. / Don't worry about it.
5. そう深刻に考えるな。 — Don't take it so seriously [hard].
6. 悲しい顔をしないで。 — Don't look so sad.

f 生徒の応答を励ます — Encouragement to speak out

TRACK 02 43

1. 九分通り正しいよ。 — You're almost right. / You've almost got it.
2. あきらめないでもう一回やってみな。 — Don't give up. [Go on.] Have another try.
3. がっかりしないで。ほぼ出来ているよ。 — Don't be discouraged. You were almost right. [Your answer was nearly completed.]
4. 気持ちを楽に。急ぐ必要はないよ。 — Take it easy. There's no need to hurry.
5. もう一回やればより良い答えが見つかるよ。 — Try again and you may find a better answer.

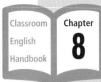

Chapter 8 あやまる
Apologizing

ⓐ 遅刻して — Being late

ア．教師が遅れて教室に入る Teacher being late 〔TRACK 02 44〕

1. ごめんね。ちょっと遅れました。 — Sorry. I'm a bit late.
2. 遅くなってごめんなさい。 — I'm sorry I'm late. / I'm sorry to be late. / I'm sorry for being late. / I apologize for being late.
3. すみません。だいぶ待ちましたか。 — Sorry. Did you wait long?
4. いや、待たせてしまった。 — Oh, you've all been waiting for me. / I'm sorry to have kept you waiting.
5. こんなに遅れてあやまります。 — I must apologize for being so late.

イ．理由の説明 Explanation 〔TRACK 02 45〕

1. バス［電車、地下鉄、（いつもの）急行］に乗り遅れました。 — I missed the bus [the train / the subway / the (usual) express].
2. バスが来ませんでした。 — The bus never came.
3. 昨夜遅くまで仕事をしていました。 — I worked till late last night.
4. 今朝、頭痛［腹痛］がしてね。 — I had a headache [a stomachache] this morning.
5. 少し気持ち悪い［目眩がする、熱がある］のです。 — I feel sick [dizzy / feverish].

b 生徒の釈明に対して　Responding to the student's apology

(((• TRACK 02 46 •)))

1. わかった。
   OK. / That's OK. / No problem. / Forget it. / That's (quite) all right. / Please don't worry.

2. 気にするな。そんなに遅くなったわけではない。
   Never mind. [Don't worry about it.] You're not so late.

c 予告なしの自習のあとで　After sudden cancellation of the class

(((• TRACK 02 47 •)))

1. 昨日は授業を休んでごめん。
   I'm sorry I cancelled the class yesterday. / I'm very sorry we had no class yesterday.

2. 熱があって［風邪をひいて］ね。
   I had a fever [a cold].

3. 義理の母の不幸がありました。
   I had to attend a funeral of my mother-in-law.

4. 夫が体調を崩して救急車で運ばれました。
   My husband was very sick and was taken to the hospital by ambulance.

d 宿題が多すぎて　Too much homework

(((• TRACK 02 48 •)))

1. 宿題は終わった？
   Have you finished your assignments?

2. 宿題が多すぎますか？
   Was [Is] it too much? / Did I give you a lot of homework [assignments]?

3. 昨夜は眠れなかった？
   Didn't you sleep at all last night?

Notes: 2で現在形の表現は宿題を出した当日、過去形は提出日の発話。アメリカでは「宿題」の意味では homework（不可算）よりも assignment（可算）が使われることが多い。

e 勘違いして — Misunderstanding

1. 失礼！
   Oops! / Sorry.
   ＊軽い失敗・へまなどに際して使う略式の表現

2. すみません。
   Excuse me. / I'm sorry.

3. あら（私の）間違いだ。
   Oh, that's a [my] mistake.

f 急用で授業を中座して — Leaving the classroom for urgent business

ア．教師の発言 Teacher

1. 少し中座します。
   Excuse me for a second [few minutes]. / You must excuse me for a moment.

2. 少しの間、中座しなければなりません。
   I have to leave the room for a couple of minutes.

イ．生徒の発言 Students

1. すみません。保健室に行かせてください。
   Excuse me. I have to go to see the nurse [go to the sickroom].

2. 席を外してもよろしいですか。
   May [Can] I be excused?

3. お手洗いに行ってもよいでしょうか。
   May I go to the rest room?

4. 11時頃、授業を中座しなければなりません。
   I have to leave the class around eleven o'clock.

Notes: 生徒が中座する時には Excuse me. と言ってからその理由を述べさせる。

感 謝

Saying Thanks

a 一般的な「ありがとう」 — Thank you

TRACK 02 52

1. ありがとう。
   ＊一般的な言い方
   Thank you (very much). / Thank you so much. / Thanks a lot [awfully].

2. ありがとう。
   ＊くだけた言い方
   Many thanks. / A thousand thanks.

3. お手伝いありがとう。
   Thanks for your help.

4. ご親切にありがとう。
   ＊一般的な言い方
   It's very kind [nice] of you.

5. ご親切にありがとうございます。
   ＊丁寧な言い方
   I appreciate your kindness.

6. 大変感謝しています。
   I'm very thankful. / I'm very grateful. / I'm very much obliged.

7. ご親切にどうも！
   How kind of you!

8. 一言お礼申し上げたい。
   I'd like to say, "Thank you."

b 手伝いに対して — For help

ア．手伝いを頼む Asking for help

TRACK 02 53

1. お手伝いお願いできますか？
   ＊丁寧さの順に
   Help me, please. / Can [Will] you help me? / Would you help me?

2. 手を貸してください。
   Lend me a hand (please).

3. 手を貸してくださいませんか。
   Would you mind helping me?

イ．生徒が手伝いを申し出る Students' offering of help 〔TRACK 02 54〕

1.	お手伝いします。	I'll help you.
2.	お手伝いしましょうか。	Can I help you? / Shall [Could] I help you?
3.	本をお持ちしましょう。	We'll carry the books for you.
4.	いいですよ。私がやりましょう。	OK. I'll do it (for you).
5.	待って。私がやります。	Wait. I'll take care of it.
6.	手を貸しましょうか。	May [Can] I lend you a hand? / Let me help you.

ウ．手伝いに感謝する Gratitude for help given 〔TRACK 02 55〕

1.	ご親切にそれをやってくれてありがとう。	It's very kind of you to do that.
2.	ありがとう。ご親切に。	Thank you very much. You are so kind.
3.	本当に助かりました。ありがとう。	You were really helpful. Thank you very much.
4.	助けていただき誠にありがとうございます。	I really do appreciate your help.
5.	おかげで多くの時間と苦労を省けました。	That saved me lots of time and trouble.

C 掃除　　Cleaning

ア．掃除の指示 Directions for cleaning 〔TRACK 02 56〕

1.	黒板を消してください。	Clean the board (please).
2.	黒板消し係は誰ですか？	Who is in charge of cleaning the blackboard?

3. 黒板消しを持ってきなさい。	Bring me that eraser.
4. 黒板を拭いてください。	Please wipe the blackboard.
5. 黒板に落書きをするな。	Don't scribble on the blackboard.
6. 教卓をきれいにしてください。	Please clean the teacher's desk.
7. この机は乱雑です。片付けてくれますか。	This desk is too messy. Will you put the things in order?

イ．掃除に感謝 Gratitude for cleaning

1. これは大変きれいですね。	This is really clean.
2. なんてきれいなの。ありがとう。	How clean! Thank you very much.
3. 黒板をきれいにしてくれてありがとう。	Thank you for cleaning the blackboard.
4. よくできました。すべてが大変きれいです。	You did a good [thorough] job. Everything is so clean.
5. 黒板がこんなにきれいで大変うれしい。	I'm very happy to see such a clean blackboard.
6. 私が来る前にすっかり整理整頓してくれてありがとう。	It's very good of you to have put everything in a good order before I came.

生徒の応答 Student Response

黒板（の字）を消して。先生が来るよ。	Hey! Wipe the blackboard. The teacher is coming.
私の当番じゃない。	It's not my duty. / Today is not my day on duty.

Chapter 9 | 感　謝

d 花などに対して　　　For flowers, etc.

(TRACK 02 58)

1. きれいですね！　　　　Beautiful!
2. きれいなお花！　　　　What pretty flowers!
3. 花をありがとう。　　　Thank you for the flowers.
4. 本当にきれいですね。　They look really beautiful, don't they?
5. 私が花瓶に入れましょう。　I'll put them in a flower pot. / Let me arrange the flowers in a vase.
6. 生け花を知っていたらなあ。　I wish I knew flower arrangement.

e プレゼントに対して　　　For the gift

(TRACK 02 59)

1. うわあ、びっくりした！ありがとう。　Oh, what a surprise! Thank you.
2. 大変驚きましたが、うれしいです。　I'm very surprised but also very happy.
3. 贈り物をありがとう。　Thank you for the present [the gift].
4. これはすばらしいプレゼントです。　This is a splendid present. / This is just beautiful [wonderful / gorgeous].
5. 皆さんとの楽しい毎日の一番の思い出として大切にします。　I'll keep it as the best memory of my happy days with you.

II 一般的指示

63

Chapter 10 生徒の発言への対応

Dealing with Students' Responses

a 誤りの訂正 — Correction of mistakes

ア．誤りを指摘する Pointing out errors (TRACK 02 60)

1. それは正しくない。
   That's not correct. / That's incorrect. / That's wrong. / You can't say that. / I'm afraid [I'm sorry] that's wrong.

2. 違う答えはありませんか？
   Can you give me another answer?

3. 誰かほかに答えることができる人は？
   Can anyone else answer?

4. 答えに自信がありますか？
   Are you sure about your answer?

5. 時間をあげます。考えてみて。
   I'll give you some time. Think about it.

6. もう一度やってごらん。
   Take your time and try again.

イ．小さな[大きな]誤り Slight [Serious] errors (TRACK 02 61)

1. ほんのわずかな誤りがある。もう1回言ってみなさい。
   Just a slight error. Say it again.

2. ほんの小さな間違いです。もう1回やってみなさい。
   It's only a small mistake. Try again.

3. 心配いりません。非常に小さな間違いです。
   Don't worry. It's a very small mistake.

4. これは重大な間違いだ。訂正しなさい。
   This is a serious mistake. Correct it.

b 場面ごとの誤りの訂正　　Correction in specific skill areas

ア．音声 Sound　　((TRACK 02 62))

1. それは正しい発音ではない。もう1回。
 : That doesn't sound right. Try again.

2. ちょっと待って。私の口を見て、もう1回言ってごらん。
 : Wait. Look at my mouth and try again.

3. 私の口の動きをよく見て、繰り返してください。
 : Please watch how my lips move and repeat after me.

4. 私の上の歯を見て。下唇に触れているでしょう。もう一度 vase と言ってごらん。
 : Look at my upper teeth. They're touching my lower lip. Say it once more 'vase'.

5. あなたの th の発音は正しくない。私の口を見て /θ/ と言って。
 : Your 'th' sound isn't correct. Look at my mouth. Say /θ/.

6. like のあとの s は /z/ とは言わない。もう一度 Tom likes pop music. と言ってごらん。
 : Don't pronounce 's' as /z/ after 'like'. Say it again 'Tom likes pop music'.

イ．文法 Grammar　　((TRACK 02 63))

1. いや、君の文には間違いがある。I go, you go, he goes だから I swim, you swim でそれから？
 : No, there's a mistake in your sentence. 'I go, you go, he goes. I swim, you swim,' then what?

2. flower のあとに何か忘れましたね。one flower, two flowers, さて3つの場合は？
 : You forgot something after the word 'flower'. One flower, two flowers and three what?

3. 「いつも朝は7時に起きる」は正しいが「食べる」に対して「食べた」で、「起きる」に対して（「起きた」は）？ | You usually get up at seven in the morning, but ... You eat, you ate... You get up, you what?

4. 'a orange' とは言わない。'an orange' となる。an apple のように。 | Don't say 'a orange'. It's 'an orange'. Say 'an apple, a banana and an ...'

ウ．綴り字・句読法 Spelling / Punctuation （TRACK 02 64）

1. ここはbです。dとbを混同してはいけません。 | This is 'b'. Don't take 'd' for 'b'.

2. あなたの書いた文の最初の文字を大文字にしなさい。 | Change the first letter of your sentence into a capital letter.

3. 文はいつも大文字で始めること。 | You must always start a sentence with a capital letter.

4. 人名や地名を小文字で始めてはいけません。 | Don't start the name of a person or a place with a small letter.

5. cutting という語にはtが2つあります。君のはtが1つしかない。 | The word 'cutting' has two t's. Yours has only one 't'.

6. あなたの書いた文には最後にピリオドがない。付けなさい。 | Your sentence has no period at the end. Add one.

7. headache の綴りが間違っています。 | You spelled 'headache' incorrectly.

8. あなたの書いた文には2つスペルミスがある。直しなさい。 | I see two spelling mistakes in your sentence. Correct them.

c 理解の確認 — Checking students' understanding

1. いいですか？ — OK? / Right?
2. わかりますか？ — Do you understand?
3. 話すのが速すぎますか？ — Am I speaking too fast?
4. 黒板に書いた文がわかりますか？ — Do you understand the sentence on the board?
5. これはわかりますか[はっきり見えますか]？ — Is this clear to you?
6. わからないのですね？ — Oh, you don't understand?
7. 繰り返してほしいですか？ — Do you want me to repeat it?

d 任意参加を求める — Eliciting students' responses

1. 誰か？ — Anyone? / Any volunteers? / Does anyone want to try? / Who wants to try?
2. さあ、誰かこの質問に答えたい人は？ — Now who wants to answer this question?
3. 誰か黒板に答えを書ける人は？ — Can anyone come to the board and write the answer?
4. 黒板にその絵を描ける人は？ — Who can draw a picture of it on the board?
5. 2人来てほしいです。 — I need two volunteers.

e 指名して反応を喚起 Eliciting responses from specific students

ア．指名 Naming students
(((• TRACK 02 67 •)))

1. 俊男、やってごらん。
   Toshio, you try.

2. 恵子、やってみませんか？
   How about you, Keiko? / Will you try, Keiko?

3. 7番の人、31ページを読んでください。
   Number seven, read page thirty-one aloud, please.

4. 俊男、黒板の所に来て、答えを書いてください。
   Toshio, please come to the blackboard and write your answer.

5. 恵子はフィオナ、和男はロバートになって対話文を読みなさい。いいですか？
   Keiko, you're going to be Fiona, and Kazuo, you'll be Robert. Now, read the dialog together, OK?

イ．反応を促す Encouragement
(((• TRACK 02 68 •)))

1. もう一度言ってください。
   Pardon? / Excuse me? / Once more, please. / Will you say it once again?

2. もう1回言ってくれませんか。今度はもっとはっきりと。
   Would you repeat that? More clearly this time, please?

3. すみません（よく聞こえませんでした）。もう一度、今度は少し高い［大きい］声で。
   Sorry? Try again and a little louder.

ウ．助け舟を出して Giving help
(((• TRACK 02 69 •)))

1. （生徒：Tom is er ...）
   トムはどんな人？
   Tom is what?

2. （生徒：I go home er ...）
   何時に帰りますか？
   You go home at what time?

3. （生徒：I couldn't do the homework, beca...）
   宿題をできなかったのはどういう理由で？

   You couldn't do the homework because of what?

4. （生徒：Yesterday I went to ...）
   昨日どこへ行きましたか？ どこへ？

   Well, where did you go yesterday? You went where?

Notes: (er)...は言葉を探して言いよどんだ場合。

6 無反応の状況で　　Dealing with silence

((• TRACK 02 70 •))

1. そんなに黙ってないで。
   Don't be so quiet.

2. 何か言いなさい。誰かいませんか。
   Well, say something. Anyone?

3. どうしてそんなに黙っているの？ 思いきって言ってみて。
   Why are you so quiet? Speak out.

4. そう恥ずかしがらないで。挙手して何か言いなさい。
   Don't be shy. Raise your hand and say something.

5. どんな答えでもいいよ。やってみて。
   Any answer is all right. Just try.

6. 間違うことを恐れないで。思いきってやってごらん。
   Don't be afraid of making mistakes. Go ahead and try.

7. 私の言っていることがわかる？ わかる？ わからない？
   Do you understand what I'm saying? Yes or no?

Chapter 11 学習活動への指示

Directions for Activities

a グループワーク — Group work

(TRACK 02 71)

1. 4人ずつの班を作りなさい。
   Form groups of four.

2. 3人ずつの班を作り、対話文を行ごとに練習しなさい。
   Practice the conversation in groups of three line by line.

3. 名前を使って自己紹介しなさい。
   Introduce each other using your names.

4. （対話文の）役を替えて全パートを練習しなさい。
   Change roles (in the dialog) so that you can practice all the parts.

5. 立ち上がって隣の人にさよならを言いなさい。
   Stand up and say good-bye to your neighbors.

6. 21ページの課題を3, 4名の班を作ってやりなさい。
   Do the exercise on page 21 in groups of three to four.

b ペアワーク — Pair work

(TRACK 02 72)

1. 交代で物を拾ってその名前をたずねなさい。
   Taking turns, pick up an object and ask its name.

2. ペアを組んで事物について質問をしたり答えたりしなさい。
   In pairs, ask and answer questions about the objects.

3. 45ページの絵について、できれば2つ質問をしなさい。

Try to ask two questions about a picture on page 45 when possible.

4. ペアで自分の好きなスポーツについて、質問と回答を交代でしなさい。

In pairs, take turns asking and answering questions about your favorite sports.

5. ペアの相手を替えて再度質問し合いなさい。

Change partners and ask your questions again.

C 聞くこと | Listening

((TRACK 02 73))

1. CDを2度聞いて、プリントの正しい答えに○をつけなさい。

Listen twice to the CD, and then circle the correct answer in your handout.

2. CDをもう一度かけるので答えをチェックしなさい。

I'll play the CD again so that you can check your answers.

3. いちごアイスクリームのレシピと作り方を聞きなさい。

Listen to the recipe and instructions for making strawberry ice cream.

4. CDをもう一度聞いて、アイスクリーム・カードを完成させなさい。

Listen to the CD again and complete the ice cream card.

5. 火星に関するお話を聞いてから回答用紙が配られます。抜けている情報を埋めなさい。

You'll hear a story about Mars, and then you'll get an answer sheet. Fill in the missing information.

d 読むこと — Reading

((• TRACK 02 74 •))

1. OHP を見て、文を読んで内容が正しいものは T，間違っているものは F と言いなさい。
   Look at the OHP screen. Read the sentences and say T for true and F for false.

2. OHP で 5 つの文を見せます。それぞれ正しいか、間違っているかを言いなさい。
   I'll show you five sentences by an OHP. Tell me which is true or false.

3. 読解の課題に制限時間を設けます。10 分以内に完成させなさい。
   I'll set a time limit for your reading task. Complete the task within ten minutes.

4. パートナーと一緒に、第 1 節にある 3 つのキーワードを見つけなさい。
   Work with a partner and find the three keywords of Section One.

5. 何人かの人に物語を音読してほしい。自分の読後感を表現できるように読んでみなさい。
   I want some of you to read the story aloud. Try to read so that you can express your feeling about the story.

e 文法 — Grammar

((• TRACK 02 75 •))

1. 文に間違いを見つけたら、その文の横に×を付けてください。
   If you find mistakes in sentences, mark an X next to the sentence.

2. 各自、練習問題を完成しなさい。答案をパートナーと交換して、確認しなさい。
   Complete the exercise individually, and then exchange your answers with a partner to check.

3. 次の対話文（の空所）にWH疑問詞を入れて、パートナーと練習しなさい。

   Fill in the following dialog with WH-questions, and then practice with your partner.

4. 絵についての3つの説明があります。どの文が正しく、どの文が間違っていますか。

   There are three descriptions of the picture. Which is correct and which is wrong?

f 語彙　　Vocabulary

((• TRACK 02 76 •))

1. 着ている衣類の名称を言いなさい。

   Identify items of clothing you're wearing.

2. パートナーと一緒に12か月の月の名前を交代で言いなさい。

   Work with a partner, and say the names of the 12 months by turns.

3. 人体絵図を見て、プリントの空欄を埋めなさい。

   You'll see an illustration of a human body. Fill in the blanks in your handout.

4. 週7日の名称を言いなさい。日曜日から始めても月曜日から始めてもよい。

   Tell me the names of the seven days of the week. You can start either from Sunday or from Monday.

5. 絵を見て絵と職種を結びつけなさい。

   Look at the pictures, and then match the pictures with the jobs.

g 子どもたちの活動　　Activities for children

1. 動物の線画にクレヨンで色をぬりなさい。

   Color these animal drawings with crayons.

2. 数字の 1, 3, 5, 7, 9 は緑に、2, 4, 6, 8, 10 は黄色にぬりなさい。

   Color the numbers 1, 3, 5, 7 and 9 green, and the numbers 2, 4, 6, 8 and 10 yellow.

3. これから 10 匹の動物の名前を言います。私が言った動物の数字を○で囲みなさい。

   I'll say the names of ten animals. Circle the numbers of the animals that I say.

4. 私と一緒に絵の中の子どもの数を左から右へと数えましょう。準備はいいですか。

   Count the children in the picture with me from left to right. Are you ready?

5. 前に出てきて、私が話す絵を指しなさい。

   Come to the front and point to the pictures that I talk about.

授業展開

Teaching Procedure

ウォームアップ
Warm-up

① 挨 拶 Greetings

a 挨 拶 — Greetings

ア．普段の挨拶 Informal greetings　（TRACK 03 01）

1. 皆さん、おはようございます。	Good morning, class [everybody / everyone / boys and girls / students].
2. 皆さんこんにちは。	Good afternoon, class [everybody / everyone / boys and girls / students]. ＊午後に　Hello. ＊時間を問わず
3. 元気ですか？	How are you? / How are you doing? / How are you getting on? / How are things (with you)? / How are you feeling today? / How's everything? / How's everyone today?
4. 変わりない？　＊くだけた言い方	How is it going?
5. どう、元気？　＊略式の挨拶	What's new? / What's up?
6. 清々しい朝ですね。	Beautiful morning, isn't it? / What a lovely morning!

Notes: 授業に入る前のウォームアップの時間は大切である。その日の挨拶を毎時間繰り返し行うことで英語に慣れてくる。6の "isn't it?" は語尾を上げて発音する。

生徒の応答 Student Response

鈴木先生、おはようございます［こんにちは］。	Good morning [Hello], Mr. Suzuki.

元気です。	I'm fine [all right / good].
とても気分がいいです。	I feel very well [great / excellent / terrific / fantastic / very good].
ひどいです。	I feel awful [terrible].
それほどよくない［まあまあ、まずまず、悪くない、よくない］です。	I feel not so good [so-so / okay / not too bad / not well].
別に。 ＊What's new? などの質問に	Nothing much. / Nothing special.
先生はどうですか？	How are you? / How about you?

イ．休み明けの挨拶　Greetings after the vacation

1. 皆さん、またよろしく。	Hello again, class. / Welcome back, everyone!
2. またお会いできてよかったです。	Nice to see you again.
3. 休暇中はどんなでしたか？	How have you been (doing)? / How was your vacation?
4. しばらく皆さんと会いませんでしたね。	I haven't seen you for a while.
5. 久しぶり！	Long time no see! ＊くだけた言い方。かなり長期にわたって会わなかった場合に
6. あけましておめでとう。 ＊3学期の初日に	Happy New Year!

生徒の応答 Student Response

とても楽しい休暇でした。	I had a great holiday [vacation].
もっと休みがあるといいです。	I wish we had more holidays.

b 生徒の反応に続けて — Respond to students' greetings

((•TRACK 03 03•))

1. 私も元気です。ありがとう。
   * How are you? に対して

   I'm fine, too. Thank you.

2. それを聞いて私も嬉しいです。

   I'm glad to hear that.

3. それはよかったです。

   That's very nice.

4. どうしましたか？
   *生徒の反応がネガティブな時

   What's wrong? / Anything wrong with you? / My goodness! / What's the matter with you? / Why is that? / What happened? / (Did) anything happen?

5. それは大変でしたね。

   Sorry to hear that. / That's too bad.

6. それについてもっと話してくれませんか？

   Can you tell me more about it?

Notes: 2, 3 は fine, great などの返事に対して。4 の My goodness! は驚きの気持ちを表す。良いことについてはあまり使わない。5 交通事故など悪いことが起こった時には What a shame [pity]! などを使うことが多い（⇒ p.56「慰め・同情」も参照）。

生徒の応答 Student Response

今日は、誕生日です。	Today is my birthday.
いいことがありましたが、それは秘密です。	Something good happened to me, but it's a secret.
風邪をひきました。	I have a cold. / I've caught (a) cold [got a cold].
昨晩、よく眠れませんでした。	I didn't sleep well last night.
昨晩は、たくさん勉強しなければなりませんでした。	I had to study too much last night.

C 時間　　　　　　　　　　　　　　　　　　　　　　Time

TRACK 03 04

1. 今、何時ですか？	What time is it now? / What time do you have? / Will you tell me the time?
2. 時計を見なさい！ ＊授業が始まっても着席しない生徒などに対して	Look at the clock!
3. 今朝は何時に起きましたか？	What time did you get up this morning?
4. 家でどのくらい勉強しますか[テレビを見ますか]？	How long do you usually study [watch TV] at home?
5. 家から学校までどのくらいかかりますか？	How long does it take from your house to school?

Notes: 英語で数字がすらすら出てくるには、普段から数字になじませる努力が大切である。3〜5のような質問を活用しよう。
例）What time do you usually leave for school?（何時に学校に行きますか？）
　　How much sleep do you get each night?（毎晩どのくらい寝ますか？）

生徒の応答 Student Response

10時45分です。	It is 10:45 [ten forty-five / a quarter to eleven].
12時30分に寝ました。	I went to bed at 12:30 [twelve-thirty / half past [after] twelve].
バスで30分かかります。	It takes thirty minutes by bus.
私の時計は3分遅れています[進んでいます]。	My watch is three minutes slow [fast].

Notes:「〜分前」は to.「〜分過ぎ」は after（アメリカ英語）/ past（イギリス英語）。

d 曜日・月日 — Days of the week [month]

{((• TRACK 03 05 •))}

1. 今日は何曜日ですか？ — What day of the week is it today?
2. 昨日は何曜日ですか？ 明日は？ — What day was it yesterday? And tomorrow?
3. 今日は何日ですか？ — What's today's date?
4. 今日は 2004 年 7 月 17 日です。 — Today is July (the) seventeenth, two thousand four.
5. 何曜日が一番好きですか？ どうして？ — What day do you like best? And why?
6. では嫌いな曜日は？ — Then what day don't you like?
7. 一番好きなテレビ番組は何ですか？ それはいつ放送されていますか？ — What TV programs do you like most? And when are they on?

Notes: what day は普通、曜日のこと。日付なら date.

生徒の応答 Student Response

もちろん、土曜日が好きです。一晩中テレビを観られます。	I like Saturday, of course! I can watch TV all night.
月曜日は気分が沈みます。	I'm never happy on Monday.

e 自己紹介 — Self-introduction

ア．教師から Teacher

{((• TRACK 03 06 •))}

1. 私の名前は、高野です。 — My name is Mr. [Ms.] Takano.

2. 今年、皆さんに英語を教えます。	I'll be teaching you English this year.
3. 皆さんはじめまして。	Nice to meet you all. / I'm glad to meet you, class.
4. 自己紹介します。	I'll [Let me] introduce myself now.
5. 皆さんの授業を週に5時間受け持ちます。	I've got five lessons a week with you.

Notes: 形式的な自己紹介ではなく気持ちのこもった挨拶の手本を示そう。3 は How do you do, class? とも言うが、形式的で old-fashioned な表現。Nice to meet you. は 2 回目以降会うときは Nice to see you. となる。

イ．生徒に自己紹介を促す Asking students to introduce themselves

((TRACK 03 07))

1. お名前は？	Your name, please. / May I have your name? / What is your name, please?
2. 自己紹介してください。	Can you tell us something about yourself?
3. お名前と学校名、そして趣味を教えてください。	Please tell your name, the name of your school and your hobby.
4. みんなに向けて1分間で自己紹介しましょう。	Please introduce yourself to all of us in one minute.

Notes: 教師やクラス全体に向かって話すだけではなく Will you introduce yourself to your neighbor?（近くの席の人に自己紹介しましょう）などと指示してもよい。またゲーム形式にするなどの工夫も考えられる。

生徒の応答 Student Response

こんにちは。私は加藤明子です。	Hello. My name is Akiko Kato.
家族や友人はアキと呼びます。皆さんもアキと呼んでください。	My family and friends call me Aki. So please call me Aki.

第一中学校の出身で、父と母と姉と私の4人家族です。	I'm from Daiichi Junior High School. There are four of us in my family, father, mother, sister and me.
よろしくお願いします。 ＊自己紹介の最後に	Nice to meet you all.

② 出欠・遅刻 Roll Call

a 出席の確認　　　　Checking attendance

((• TRACK 03 08 •))

1. 出欠を取ります。　　(I'll do the) roll-call. / I'll call the roll.
2. 名前を呼びます。　　I'm going to call your names.
3. 名前を呼ばれたら here と言いなさい。　　When I call your name, please say "here."
4. 全員いますか？　　Is everybody here?
5. 欠席者は誰？　　Who is absent [missing / not here] today?
6. 全員出席してくれてうれしいです。　　I'm glad that everyone is here.

生徒の応答 Student Response

はい。	Here. ＊一般的 / Present. ＊ややFormal
いえ、私の名前はコジマではなくオジマです。	No. My name is Ojima, not Kojima.
保健室に行きました。	She went to (see) the nurse.
早退しました。	He went back home.

b 欠席［遅刻］の理由　Reasons for being absent [late]

ア．欠席の理由　Reasons for being absent　　TRACK 03 09

1. 風邪を引いたのですか？ — Did you have a cold?
2. 病気でしたか？ — Have you been ill? / Were you sick?
3. もう平気ですか？ — Are you okay [all right] now?
4. もうよくなりましたか？ — Are you feeling better now?
5. 先週はなぜ休んだのですか？ — Why were you absent last week?
6. 今日はあなたに会えてよかったです。 — I'm glad to see you today.

Notes:「具合が悪い」はアメリカ英語では sick, イギリス英語では ill. sick はイギリス英語では「吐きそう」という意味で使われることが多い。

生徒の応答　Student Response

風邪を引きました。	I had a cold.
腹痛でした。	I had a stomachache.
寝込んでいました。	I was sick in bed.
祖母のお葬式でした。	It was my grandmother's funeral.
バスケ部の試合でした。	Our basketball team had a game.
入学試験を受けました。	I took the entrance exam.

イ．遅刻の理由　Reasons for being late　　TRACK 03 10

1. どうして遅刻したのですか？ — Why so late? / Why are you late? / How come you were so late? / Tell me why you are late. / What made you come so late?

2. どこにいたのですか？	Where have you been?
3. 今来たのですか？	Have you just arrived?

Notes: 教師が遅刻の理由を追及するより、生徒が I'm sorry to be late. のあとに簡単に理由を英語で述べるという習慣をつけたほうが両者にとって気持ちがよい。

生徒の応答 Student Response

〈遅刻した本人が〉	
遅刻してすみません。	I'm sorry I'm late. / Please forgive me for being late.
始業ベルが聞こえませんでした。すみません。	I'm sorry I didn't hear the bell.
今朝寝坊をしました。	I got up late this morning.
バスに乗り遅れました。	I missed the bus.
担任の先生に呼ばれていました。	I had to see my homeroom teacher.
〈遅刻した友人に〉	
どうしたの？	What happened?
大丈夫？	Are you OK?
あのバスはいつも遅れるんだ。	The bus is always late.

ウ．注意 Admonition

((TRACK 03 11))

1. 二度と遅れてはいけません。	Don't be late (ever) again.
2. 時間どおりに来なさい。いいね？	Be here on time. OK?
3. 急いで座って。授業は始まっています。	Hurry up and sit down. We've already started.

4. 気にしないで、誰にでもあることだから。	Never mind. It can happen to anyone.
5. それは大変でしたね。もう大丈夫ですか。	Oh, that's too bad. Are you all right now?

Notes: 4, 5 はやむをえない事情で遅れた生徒に対して。

生徒の応答 Student Response

すみません。もう二度と遅刻しません。約束します。	I'm sorry. I'll never be late again. I promise.
僕のせいじゃありません。	It's not my fault.

C 健康状態を気遣う Showing concern about students' well-being

TRACK 03 12

1. 今朝は皆さん元気ですか？	Are you all well this morning?
2. 最近、風邪をひく人が多いです。気をつけて。	Many people catch cold these days. Take care.
3. 武男はまだ欠席ですね。風邪ですか？	Takeo is still absent today. Does he have a cold?
4. もどって来ましたね。よかった。もう大丈夫ですか？	Oh, you're back. That's good. Are you feeling better now?

Notes: 具合の悪そうな生徒がいたら Are you all right? などと声をかけよう。症状を表す表現は次のとおり。
例）「顔色が悪いです」You look pale. /「顔が赤いです」You look flushed. /
　　「汗をかいています」You're sweating.

生徒の応答 Student Response

大丈夫です。	I'm all right. / No problem. / Never mind. / That's OK.
具合が悪いです。	I don't feel well.
あまり具合がよくないですが、大丈夫です。	I don't feel very well, but it's OK [I'm all right].

③ 天候 Weather

a 晴れ — Fine

((• TRACK 03 13 •))

1. 天気がいいですね。 — Nice day, isn't it? / It's [The weather is] fine today, isn't it?
2. いい天気です。 — It's such a beautiful day! / What a sunny day! / It's a great day!
3. ついに晴れてよかったです。
    ＊長く続いた雨のあとで
    — I'm glad to see the sun at last.

b 曇り — Cloudy

((• TRACK 03 14 •))

1. 今日は曇りです。 — It's cloudy today.
2. 雨が降りそう。 — I'm afraid it will rain soon.
3. なんてうっとうしい日だろう。 — What a gloomy [gray] day!
4. 空を見て。大きな黒い雲です！ — Look at the sky. What a big black cloud!

Chapter 1 | ウォームアップ

c 雨 — Rainy

TRACK 03 15

1.	雨が降っています。	It's raining. / It's rainy today. / It looks like rain.
2.	雨が激しく降っています。	It's pouring rain. / It's pouring down.
3.	雨にはうんざりします。	I'm so tired of rain.
4.	あ、雨だ。皆さん傘は持ってきましたか？	Oh, it has started to rain. Did you bring your umbrellas with you?

Notes: 一度やんで降り始めた時にはIt's raining again today.「また雨か」はAnother wet day! 4は一人に言う場合はumbrella.

d 暖かい — Warm

TRACK 03 16

1.	今日は暖かいです。	It's warm today.
2.	春が来ました。	Spring has come.
3.	いい季節ですね。私は本当に春が好きです。	Isn't it a beautiful season? I really love spring.
4.	今日は、暖かくて気持ちがいいです。	Today it's warm and comfortable.
5.	あまりに気持ちの良い天気で、眠くなります。	The weather is too comfortable. I'm getting sleepy.
6.	皆さんが寝てしまうんじゃないかと心配です。	I'm afraid you'll get sleepy [fall asleep].
7.	天気はすぐに変わるので、風邪をひかないよう注意してください。	The weather changes quickly. Be careful not to catch cold.

Ⅲ 授業展開

Notes: 「昨日よりかなり暖かい」は It's much warmer than yesterday.「暖かくなってきた」は It's getting warmer.

e 暑い   Hot

TRACK 03 17

1. 今日はとても暑いです。 — It's very hot today.
2. どうして毎日こう暑いのでしょうか。 — Why is it so hot every day?
3. 暑い日が続きますね。 — Another hot day, isn't it?
4. 毎日だんだん暑くなっています。 — It's getting hotter every day.

Notes: 1「少し暑い」は a little hot. とても暑い場合には、terribly hot（ひどく暑い）/ awfully hot（恐ろしく暑い）/ boiling hot（焼け付くように暑い）など。

f 蒸し暑い   Humid

TRACK 03 18

1. 今日は蒸し暑いです。 — It's hot and humid. / It's very sticky.
2. どうして今日はこんなに蒸し暑いのでしょうか。 — Why is it so muggy today?
3. 皆さん暑くて汗ばんでいるようです。 — You all look so hot and sweaty.

生徒の応答 Student Response

| 暑くて勉強できない。 | It's too hot to study. |

夏バテです。	I can't cope with the summer heat.
勉強するエネルギーがありません。	I have no energy to study.
体育の授業だったんです。 ＊汗をかいていると言われて	The last class was PE.

g 寒い　　　　　　　　　　　　　　　　　　Cold

((• TRACK 03 19 •))

1. 今日は寒いです。	It's cold today.
2. 今朝はじつに寒いです。	It sure is cold this morning.
3. 身が引き締まるようにさわやかです。	It's cool and crisp.
4. 外は晴れているけど、肌寒いです。	It's sunny outside, but it's chilly.
5. とても寒いから自分の息が見えます。	It's so cold (that) you can see your breath.

Notes: 1「凍えるように寒い」は freezing cold.「日に日に寒くなってきている」は It's getting colder every day. 5 は日本語で言うところの「吐く息が白く見える」。

生徒の応答 Student Response

暖房［ストーブ］が入るのはいつからですか？	When will we get a heater [stove]?
職員室は暖房をつけています。私たちも暖房をつけましょう。	You have heaters on in the teachers' room. Why don't we have them on?

h 霜・氷 — Frost / Ice

TRACK 03 20

1. この季節の初氷ですね。　　The first ice of the season.
   ＊凍りついた窓外を指して
2. 今朝は霜を見ましたか？　　Did you see the frost this morning?
3. 昨晩はひどい霜でした。　　There was a heavy frost last night.
4. 窓を見て。霜で白くなっています。　　Look at the window. It's white with frost.
5. 学校の池が凍っているのに気づきましたか？　　Did you notice the school pond is frozen?

i 雪 — Snow

TRACK 03 21

1. ひっきりなしに雪が降っています。　　It's snowing fast.
2. 外を見て！　雪だ！　　Look outside! Snow!
3. 雪が降っています。とてもきれい。　　Look at the snow falling. How beautiful!
4. 毎日雪ばかり。　　Snow, snow every day.
5. 吹雪だ！　　What a blizzard! / What a snowstorm!
6. 雪はどのくらい深いですか？　　How deep is the snow?
7. 3日間［月曜日から］ずっと雪が降り続いています。　　It has been snowing for three days [since Monday].

Notes:「ひどく降る」It's snowing heavily. /「少し降る」It's snowing a little [lightly].

④ 前日[先週]の話題 Topics of the Preceding Day [Week]

ⓐ 普段の生活　　　　　　　　　　　　　　　　　Everyday life

ア．家庭生活　Home [Family] life　　　　　　🔊 TRACK 03 22

1. いつも何時に寝ますか［起きますか］？	What time do you usually go to bed [get up]?
2. 今朝の朝食は何でしたか？	What did you have for breakfast this morning?
3. 昨日、何をしていたか教えてください。	Tell me what you did yesterday.
4. 趣味は？	What is your hobby?
5. ペットを飼っていますか。どんな動物？	Do you have a pet? What kind of animal is it?
6. 家で両親の手伝いをしますか？　何をしますか？	Do you help your parents at home? What do you do?

Notes: 楽しい話題を選んでくつろいだ話が英語でできると、教師と生徒の間に信頼関係（rapport）が生まれる。

生徒の応答 Student Response

趣味は野球［読書］です。	My hobby is baseball [reading].
私はスポーツが好きです。	I like sports [doing sports].
いつか旅行［山登り］がしたいです。	I wish to travel [climb mountains] someday.

イ．学校生活　School life　　　　　　🔊 TRACK 03 23

1. どうやって学校に来ていますか？	How do you come to school?

2.	どの科目が一番好きですか？	What subject do you like most [best]?
3.	ではどの科目が嫌いですか？　なぜ？	Then what subject don't you like? Why?
4.	担任の先生は誰ですか？	Who is your homeroom teacher?
5.	どんなクラブに入っていますか？　楽しい？	What club do you belong to? Do you enjoy it?

Notes: 勉強が苦手でも、クラブで一生懸命やっていることを誇りにしている生徒は多い。生徒の好きな話題を出してコミュニケーションを図る。

生徒の応答 Student Response

国語［数学］が好きです。	I like Japanese [math].
数学が好きではありません。それは難しい［ややこしい、退屈だ、面白くない］からです。	I don't like math, because it's too difficult [complicated / boring / not interesting].

ウ．社会生活 Social life

(((• TRACK 03 24 •)))

1.	毎日、新聞を読みますか？	Do you read the newspaper every day?
2.	どんなニュースに興味がありますか？	What news [current events] are you interested in?
3.	私の家の近くで昨晩、自動車の事故がありました。痛ましいことです。	There was a car accident last night near my house. It was terrible.
4.	昨日の夜のNHKのドキュメンタリーを観ましたか？　とても面白い番組でした。	Did you watch the NHK documentary last night? It was a very interesting program.

Notes: 2. news は新聞やテレビでのニュース。current events は社会で起こっている出来事など広い意味。

生徒の応答 Student Response

私はいつも［時々］新聞を読みます。	I always [sometimes] read a newspaper.
新聞は読みません。	I never read a newspaper.

b 週の始め・休暇明け　　Earlier part of the week

((• TRACK 03 25 •))

1. 週末［休暇］はどうでしたか？　　How was your weekend [holiday]?
2. よい週末でしたか？　　Did you have a good weekend [enjoy your weekend]?
3. この週末は何をしましたか？　　What did you do over the weekend?
4. 昨日は出かけましたか？家にいましたか？　　Did you go out or stay at home yesterday?

生徒の応答 Student Response

休暇中はほぼ毎日学校に来て、ブラスバンド・コンクールの練習をしました。	During the vacation I came to school almost every day to practice for a coming brass band contest.
泳ぐ時間はありませんでした。	I didn't have time to swim.
お盆に家族で温泉に行きました。	During *Obon*, I went to a hot spring with my family.
家族と楽しい時間を過ごしました。	I had a good time with my family.

授業展開

C 週の終わり頃 — Latter part of the week

TRACK 03 26

1. 明日は休日です。 — Tomorrow is a holiday.
2. ついに金曜日です。 — Friday at last! / Thank God, it's Friday!
3. 今週は長かったですね。 — This week was very long, wasn't it?
4. 今週はどうでしたか？ — How was this week for you?
5. 明日は外出しますか、1日中家にいますか？ — Will you go out or rest at home all day tomorrow?
6. 学校が始まって最初の週ですから、お疲れでしょう。 — You must be tired (now), because this is the first week of school.
7. 明日は土曜日ですが、模擬試験があります。お気の毒ですが頑張ってください。 — Tomorrow is Saturday. But you have a practice exam. I'm sorry about it. Good luck!
8. 今日は週の最後の授業です。リラックスして英語の歌を聞きましょう。 — Today is the last class of the week. Let's relax and listen to an English song.

Chapter 2 復習
Review

① 宿題の提出 Handing in Homework

a 係が集める　　Students in charge of collecting

TRACK 03 27

1. では、宿題を集めます。 ＊集めるように身ぶりで示す	Now, homework.
2. 宿題を絵美さんに。早くしなさい。	All your homework to Emi-san. Hurry up.
3. 誰が宿題を集めますか？	Who collects homework? / Who's going to collect homework?
4. 陽子なの。彼女に渡してください。 ＊3に続けて	Is it you, Yoko? Pass your papers to her, please.
5. 今すぐに集め始めてください。	Start collecting right now.
6. 今日の宿題係は誰？	Who is in charge of (collecting) homework [the assignment] today?

Notes: 6 英語には「〜係」に相当する単語がない。in charge of を使う。また、提出物を受け取る時、日本人教師は無言のことも多いが、英語圏では生徒に対しても Thank you. と言うのが普通。

生徒の応答 Student Response

宿題を集めるのは今ですか、後ですか？	Do we collect homework now or later?
いつ宿題を先生のところへ持っていきますか？	When do we bring homework to you?

雅男を抜かしていいですか？　彼は今日欠席です。	Can we skip Masao's? He is absent today.

b 列ごとに集める — Collecting by row

TRACK 03 28

1. 宿題を送ってください。
   ＊手の動きで指示

   Pass them [it] in.

2. 宿題を前の人に送って。

   Pass the papers forward.

3. 席を離れないで、前の人に渡してください。

   Don't leave your seat. Just pass it to the person in front of you.

4. 各列の一番後ろの席の人は立ち上がってノートを集めてください。

   The students at the end of each row, will you please stand up and collect the notebooks?

c 教卓に出す — Bringing homework to the teacher's desk

TRACK 03 29

1. 宿題を私の机に置きにきてください。

   (Put it) here on my desk.
   ＊宿題を集めているのが明確な状況で

   Come and put your assignment on my desk.

2. 宿題はここへ。

   Leave your work here.

3. 皆さん、ノートを見せにきてください。

   Everyone, come and show your notebooks to me.

d 授業後に提出 — Handing in after the class is over

((TRACK 03 30))

1. 授業後に提出してください。 — Give it to me after class.
2. 退出する前に宿題を提出してください。 — Hand in your assignment before you leave.
3. 授業が終わったら、宿題を集めます。 — I'd like to collect your homework after the class.

生徒の応答 Student Response

レポートを忘れました。明日提出できますか？	I forgot my paper. Can I hand it in tomorrow? ＊paper＝レポート；英国では「試験の答案」
宿題が終わっていません。あとで先生の部屋へ持って行っていいですか？	I have not done the homework yet. May I bring it later to your room?

② 宿題の発表 Presentation and Checking of Homework

a 口頭で — Orally

((TRACK 03 31))

1. （宿題の）回答を発表してください。 — Tell us your answers to the questions (for the homework).
2. こちらに来て（宿題の）答えを読み上げなさい。 — Come here and read aloud the answers (for the homework).
3. 書いてきたことを順番に読み上げましょう。 — Let's take turns to read aloud what you have written.

b 板書で — On the (black)board

TRACK 03 32

1. ここに書いてください。 — Write it here.
2. 1番の答えの横［下］に書いてください。 — Write it next to [below] answer No. 1.
3. チョークを取って、そこに答えを書きなさい。 — Take a piece of chalk and write the answer there.
4. 黒板のところに来て、答えを書きなさい。 — Come to the board and write your answers.
5. 黒板に答え［例］を書きます。 — I'll write the answers [the examples] on the board.

Notes: 5 は教師が正しい答えを板書する場合。板書の指示は⇒ p.125。OHP を使って発表する場合は⇒ p.121

c 隣の人と宿題チェック — Checking with neighbors each other's homework

TRACK 03 33

1. 友達と答えを確かめてください。 — Check the answers with your friend.
2. 隣の人と宿題の用紙を交換して。 — Exchange your homework sheets with your neighbors.
3. 隣の人の宿題に間違いがないか確認しなさい。 — Check for errors in your neighbor's assignment(s).
4. お互いの作文を確認してください。 — Let's check each other's compositions.
5. ペアになって、用紙を見せ合ってください。 — Work in twos [pairs] and show your sheets to each other.

Chapter 2 | 復 習

③ 暗唱文の確認 Checking Memorized Key Sentences

a 口頭英作文として As an oral composition

((• TRACK 03 34 •))

1. 英語で言いなさい。　　　　　　Say it in English.

2. 口頭で練習をしましょう。　　　Let's do some oral practice.

3. 目標文を暗記しました。もう一度言ってもらいましょう。　　You have memorized the target sentence. I want to hear you say it again.

4. キーとなる文を暗記しましたね。　　You have learned the key sentence by heart, haven't you?

5. キーとなる文をちょっと変えて言ってください。　　Let's change the key sentence slightly and say it.

生徒の応答 Student Response

教科書は閉じたままですか？	Textbooks closed?
教科書を見たいです。	I want to look at my textbook.
間違っているかもしれないけど…	There may be something wrong, but…

b 対話形式で In dialog

((• TRACK 03 35 •))

1. 立ち上がって対話をしてみてください。　　Stand up and do [have] the dialog, please.

2. それを会話形式で言ってみましょう。　　Let's say [practice] it in a dialog.

3.	キーとなる文を使って寸劇をしましょう。	Let's do the skit using the key sentences.
4.	あなたはメアリーの役で、私はジャックです。	You play Mary's role. I will play Jack's part.
5.	では男子が質問をして、女子は答えなさい。	Now, boys, ask the questions. Girls, answer them.

c 一人で — By oneself

(((• TRACK 03 36 •)))

1.	幸代、文を読みなさい。	Read the sentence, Sachiyo.
2.	一人で読めますか？	Can you read it by yourself?
3.	この列の人、順番に一文ずつ読みなさい。	This row, take turns and read it one by one.
4.	もう一回、少し早く言ってみなさい。	Say it again. And try to say it a little faster.
5.	前回の課の目標文は何でしたか？	What was the target sentence of the last lesson?
6.	皆さん、それを一緒に読んではいけません。一人ずつどうぞ。 ＊一斉に読もうとするのを遮って、一人ずつ読ませる時に	Don't read it in chorus, class. One person at a time, please.

d 意味を考えて — Thinking of the meaning of the sentences

(((• TRACK 03 37 •)))

1.	それを読んで、意味を考えなさい。	Read it and think of the meaning.

2.	これはどういう意味ですか？	What does this mean?
3.	最初に意味をよく考えて。それから読み始めなさい。	First, think hard about the meaning. Then, start reading.
4.	文を理解できましたか？ よろしい、では読んで。	Do you understand the sentence? OK. Then read it.
5.	口頭練習はよくできましたが、意味はわかっていますか？	You did a good job on [with] the oral practice. But are you sure of its meaning?

生徒の応答 Student Response

cruel の意味を忘れました。	I forgot the meaning of 'cruel'.
parent の意味は何ですか？	What does 'parent' mean?

e 気持ちを込めて — Expressing your feeling

TRACK 03 38

1.	気持ちを込めて読んでください。	Read it with emotion [feeling].
2.	もっと気持ちを込めて。	More emotion, please. / With more emotion!
3.	これは感嘆文ですから。 ＊2 に続けて	Because this is an exclamatory sentence.
4.	ジェスチャーも付けて読んでください。	Read it with some gestures.
5.	もっとゆっくり読みなさい。 ＊内容を考えないで一気に読んでしまう生徒に対して	Read it much more slowly.

Ⅲ 授業展開

④ 前時のテキスト Last Lesson

a 要約 Summary

(((• TRACK 03 39 •)))

1. その節をもう一度見ましょう。何が書いてありますか？
   Let's look at the passage once again. What does it say?

2. 文章の大意を自分の言葉で言いなさい。
   Explain the outline of the text in your own words.

3. その部分の短い要約を言ってみなさい。
   Give me a brief summary of it.

生徒の応答 Stuent Response

うまく要約できません。	I can't summarize it well.
要約するのにもっと時間をください。	Give me more time to summarize.

b 主人公の行動 What the characters in the story did

(((• TRACK 03 40 •)))

1. 最後の段落でラッシーは何をしましたか？
   What did Lassie do in the last paragraph?

2. つうは実は鶴だったのです。よひょうがそれに気づいたとき、何が起こりましたか。
   Tsu was a crane in fact. When Yohyo found it, what happened?

3. 本文で「トムには良い考えがあった」とありますが、それは何でしたか？
   The text says, "Tom had a good idea." What was it?

Notes: テキストの中の主人公の行動などを確認する時に使う。

生徒の応答 Student Response

その登場人物の気持ちがわかりません。	I can't understand the feelings of this person.
なぜ彼はそんなことをした［言った］のだろうか？	Why did he do [say] such a thing?

C 対話の理解 — Understanding of the dialog

TRACK 03 41

1. What's up? とはどういう意味ですか？	What does "What's up?" mean?
2. I'm a stranger here. は日本語でどういう意味ですか？	How do you say "I'm a stranger here." in Japanese?
3. このスキットでスティーブは I feel blue. と言いましたが、ここでは blue はどういう意味で使われていますか？	In this skit, Steve said, "I feel blue." In what sense is the word "blue" used here?

Notes: 対話の解釈の確認をするための表現である。

生徒の応答 Student Response

これは口語表現ですか？	Is this spoken English?
これは会話で使いますか？	Can we use this in conversation?
これは、くだけた文に使ってもいいですか？	Can we use it in informal sentences?

導 入
Introduction

① 重要構文 Important Constructions

a 意味 Meaning

ア．日本語で意味をとらえさせる Through Japanese　(((・TRACK 03 42・)))

1. この文はどういう意味ですか？ — What does this sentence mean? / What is the meaning of this sentence?
2. 日本語では？ — In Japanese?
3. その文を日本語に訳してください。 — Put the sentence into Japanese.
4. この語はどういう意味ですか？ — What does this word stand for? / What does this word mean?

生徒の応答 Student Response

これが主語でしょう？	This is the subject, isn't it? / Is this the subject?
動詞はどれですか？	Which (word) is the verb? / Where is the verb?

イ．聞いてその文の内容を考えさせる Listening for meaning

(((・TRACK 03 43・)))

1. この絵を見て、よく聞きなさい。 — Look at this picture, and listen carefully.
2. she は誰ですか？ 彼女は何をしたいのですか？ — Who is 'she'? What does she want to do?
3. この男の子は彼女を知っていますか？ — Does this boy know her?

4. その少女は泣いています。なぜ泣いているのでしょうか。	The little girl is crying. Tell me why she is crying.

b 表現形式　　Forms

(((• TRACK 03 44 •)))

1. この部分を注意深く見てください。	Look at this part carefully.
2. その文で何か新しいことがありますか？	Do you see anything new in the sentence?
3. 1つ皆さんに教えていないことを含んでいます。	It contains [There's] one thing I haven't taught you yet.
4. これらの単語はすべて同じ語尾です。どういう意味でしょうか？ ＊語尾変化に注目させる時	These words all have the same endings. What do they mean?

c 読み方　　Oral reading

(((• TRACK 03 45 •)))

1. 上から［下から］4行目を読んで。	Read the fourth line from the top [the bottom].
2. このページの目標文を暗記しなさい。	Try to memorize target sentences on this page.
3. その文をあなたの隣の人を相手に読みなさい。	Read the sentences to your partner [neighbor].
4. 最初にその文を黙読し、それを見ないで声に出して言ってみなさい。	First, read the sentence silently, then say it aloud from memory [without looking at it].

| 5. この文は読みにくいです。 | This sentence is rather difficult to read. |

Notes: 生徒の読み方に注意を促す際の指示は⇒ p.46。内容や状況を考えて読むときの指示は⇒ p. 47

d 言い換え — Paraphrasing

((• TRACK 03 46 •))

| 1. このように言うこともできます。 | You can say it this way. |
| 2. 同じ内容をこのように言うこともできます。 | The same meaning is expressed in this way, too. |

② 演示による導入 Introduction by Demonstration

a 教師の動作 — By the teacher

((• TRACK 03 47 •))

1. 私のするように動いて。	Do as I do. / Follow me like this.
2. よく聞いて私のことをよく見てください。	Listen and look at [watch] me carefully.
3. 私は何をしていますか？	What am I doing?
4. 私はどこへ行きますか？	Where am I going?
5. 私の手と足がどう動くか見ていて。	See how my arms and legs move.
6. 彼らが何をしているか言いなさい。	Tell me what they're doing.

b 生徒の動作 — By the student

TRACK 03 48

1. もっと大きな身振りをしなさい。
   Give a bigger gesture.
2. 私の言っていることを聞いて、すぐに身振りで表現しなさい。
   Listen to my words and make a gesture quickly.
3. 弘美が演技をします。彼女が何をしているか言ってみなさい。
   Hiromi will make an action. Say what she is doing.

c 動作の指示 — Directing students' actions

TRACK 03 49

1. あなたの頭に［額に］触れなさい。
   Touch your head [forehead].
2. あなたの親指［人差し指］を上げなさい。
   Lift your thumb(s) [forefinger(s)].
3. 天井を見なさい。
   Look up at the ceiling.
4. 目を閉じなさい［開けなさい］。
   Close [Open] your eyes.
5. 机といすを向こうに向けなさい。
   Turn your desk and chair around.
6. パートナーの右肩を軽くたたきなさい。
   Tap your partner's right shoulder. / Pat your partner on the right shoulder.
7. 拍手をしなさい。
   Clap your hands.

d 2つの動作の相違 By showing difference(s) between the two patterns [behaviors]

TRACK 03 50

1. 私をよく見て。何か違いがわかりますか？
   : Look at me carefully. Do you see any difference?

2. 彼らを見て。雅子は何をしていて、寛子は何をしていますか？
   : Look at them. What is Masako doing and what is Hiroko doing?

3. 私の腕は上がっていますか、下がっていますか？
   : Is my arm up or down?

4. あなたは、座っていますか、立っていますか？
   : Are you sitting or standing?

e 役割指定 By role plays

ア．役割を教師が指定 Roles to be assigned by the teacher

TRACK 03 51

1. あなたは先生になりなさい。
   : You will play the teacher.

2. 誰かが佐藤先生の役をやります。やりたい人？
   : Someone must play the part of Mr. Sato. Does anyone want to do?

3. この役には治夫がふさわしい。
   : Haruo is good [suitable] for this character.

イ．グループ内で生徒同士が役割決定 Roles to be assigned by students

TRACK 03 52

1. 自分たちで話し合って役割を決めなさい。
   : Talk among yourselves and decide on the parts.

2. それぞれの登場人物についてよく考えなさい。
   : I'd like you to think hard about each character.

③ 新出語 New Words

a 発音　Pronunciation

TRACK 03 53

1. よく聞いて繰り返しなさい。　　Listen carefully and repeat.
2. CDを聞いて、繰り返してください。　　Please listen to the CD and repeat after it.
3. 最初によく聞きなさい。繰り返そうとしないでください。　　First, listen very carefully. Don't try to repeat.

b 意味　Meaning

ア．実物を使って　By actual objects

TRACK 03 54

1. これは何ですか？　　What's this?
2. これは英語で何と言いますか？　　What's the English word for this?

イ．絵を使って　By pictures

TRACK 03 55

1. 絵の中の少女は、歌って［踊って］います。　　The girl in the picture is singing [dancing].
2. 彼らは何をしていますか？　　Can you tell what they are doing?

ウ．英語で　Through English

TRACK 03 56

1. よく聞いて。英語でその語を説明します。　　Listen carefully. I will explain the word in English.

2.	語の意味を推測してください。英語で言いますよ。	Please guess the meaning of the word. I will say it in English.
3.	辞書を使わずに意味を推測しなさい。	Try to guess the meaning, without using a dictionary.

c フラッシュカードで — By flashcards

TRACK 03 57

1.	カードを見て。単語を一緒に読みましょう。	Look at the cards. Read the words all together.
2.	単語を読めますか？	Can you read the words?
3.	（カードに書かれている）それぞれの語を正確に［素早く］発音してください。	Please pronounce each word correctly [quickly].

d 連語 — Collocations

TRACK 03 58

1.	3つの語を一緒に覚えなさい。	Remember all the three words together.
2.	この句のあとにいつもatがきます。	"At" usually comes after this phrase.
3.	一度結びつくと、これらの単語はまったく違った意味になります。	Once combined, these words mean very different things.
4.	それらの単語を結びつけて覚えなさい。	You should remember those words in combination.

e 同音異義語 — Homonyms

((TRACK 03 59))

pair と pear は同じ発音ですが、綴りと意味は違います。	"Pair" and "pear" sound the same, but they are different in spelling and meaning.

④ 本文・対話 Main Text and Dialog

a 要点 — Summarizing

((TRACK 03 60))

1. 要約すると、その段落は、農家はネズミを捕まえるためにネコを飼っていたことを述べています。
   In short, the paragraph says that farmers kept cats to catch mice.

2. 自分の言葉でメアリーについて教えなさい。
   Use your own words to tell me about Mary.

3. 本文の要点は簡潔に言うと何ですか？
   In short, what is the main point of the text?

4. その節について簡単な英語で話します。
   I'll tell you about the passage in simple English.

Notes: 要点を把握させる場合は、できるだけやさしい英語で行う。「段落の大意」(p.135) も参照。

b 質問 — Asking questions

((TRACK 03 61))

1. では質問です。
   Now, questions.

2. 質問に答えてください。
   Answer the questions.

3.	皆さんが理解したか確認しましょう。	Let's see if you've understood.
4.	その一節について質問しましょう。	Let's ask some questions about [on] the passage.
5.	5つの質問があります。本文にしたがって答えてください。	There are five questions. Answer them according to the text.

C 登場人物の相互関係　　Relation between the characters

1.	何人の登場人物がこの話には出てきますか？	How many people [characters] are in the story?
2.	主人公は誰ですか？	Who is the hero [the heroine] of the story?
3.	同じ家族の中にはほかに誰がいますか？	Who else are in the same family?
4.	ジョンとメアリーはどんな関係ですか？	What's the relationship between John and Mary?
5.	エミとマイクはどのようにして知り合いましたか？	How did Emi and Mike know each other?

Chapter 4 練 習

Practice

① 語と文 Words and Sentences

a 強 勢 — Stress / Accent

(((• TRACK 04 01 •)))

1. récord と言ってください。 — Please say "récord", "récord."
2. recórd ではなく récord です。 — Say "récord", not "recórd."
3. もう一度。 — Say once again, "récord."

Notes: 強勢については p.133 も参照。

b イントネーション — Intonation

(((• TRACK 04 02 •)))

1. 文末で声を上げましょう［下げましょう］。 — Please raise [lower] your voice at the end.
2. 繰り返して。「トムは学生ですか？」 — Repeat after me, "Is Tom a student?"
3. これは二者択一の［選択］疑問文です。もう一度聞きなさい。 — This is an A-or-B [alternative] question. Listen to me again.
4. WH 疑問文です。文末で声を上げません。 — It's a WH-question. Don't raise your voice at the end.

5. 繰り返して、「私の好きな科目は英語、国語、音楽と体育です」。	Repeat after me, "My favorite subjects are English, Japanese, music and PE."

Notes: イントネーションは、板書や手による指示も与えることで、よりはっきり理解させることができる（⇒ p.132）。5は3つ以上の語を例示する時のイントネーション。

c 例文　　　　　　　　　　　　　　Example sentences

((• TRACK 04 03 •))

1. 例文を読んでください、俊男。	Please read the model sentence, Toshio.
2. 一斉に例文を読んでください。	Please read the model sentence in chorus.
3. もう1つの例を挙げてください、恵子。	Give me another example, Keiko.
4. もう1文書いてください。	Write one more sentence, please.
5. 私が例を挙げます。繰り返してください。	I'll give you an example. Repeat after me.
6. 2, 3分あげます。例文を暗記してください。	I'll give you a few minutes. Please memorize the model sentence.

d ルックアップ・アンド・セイ　　　　Look up and say

((• TRACK 04 04 •))

1. 皆さん、一度その文を音読して。それから顔を上げて言ってください。	Everybody, please read the sentence aloud once, then look up and say it.

2. ノートを見ないで。顔を上げて言ってください。
Don't read from your notebook. Look up and say it, please.

3. ではパートナーの顔を見なさい。教科書を読んではいけません。
Look at your partner now. Don't read from the textbook.

Notes: Look up and say は、まず例文や語句などを理解、暗唱し、そのあと顔を上げて話し相手を見ながら話すように言うことである。

e 綴り | Spelling

(((• TRACK 04 05 •)))

1. その単語の綴りを書いてください。
Please spell out the word.

2. その単語の綴りを読んでください。
Read the spelling of the words, please.

3. 辞書を使ってその単語の綴りを確認してください。
Please check the spelling of the word with your dictionary.

4. 皆さん、健の綴りは正しいですか？
Class, is Ken's spelling correct?

5. 5回その単語の綴りを書いて覚えなさい。
Write the spelling of the word five times and memorize it.

6. 文の最初は大文字で始めましょう。
Start a sentence with a capital letter.

7. 英語で「熱心な」は何と言いますか？ 綴りを書いてみて。
How do you say *Nesshinna* in English? Spell out the word, please.

② 文型練習 Pattern Practice

a 代入　Substitution drill

(((• TRACK 04 06 •)))

1. 単語を与えられた語を使って書き換えなさい。

   Change the words with the cues.

2. 「私は教師です」「あなたは生徒です」。では皆で一緒に。「俊男は生徒です」。

   "I am a teacher." "You are a student." Everybody together. "Toshio is a student."

Notes: 文型練習は、1のような機械的な指示はできるだけ避けて、2で示したように教師の問いかけで自然に生徒が了解していくのがいい。なるべく実際の状況を利用し、実感のある例文で練習するよう配慮したい。

b 語順転換　Inversion drill

(((• TRACK 04 07 •)))

1. これを疑問文にしなさい。

   Change [Put] this into the question form.

2. 「あなたは英語が好きです」。これを疑問文に直します。

   "You like English." Change this into a yes or no question.

c 文転換　Conversion drill

(((• TRACK 04 08 •)))

1. 文を書き換えなさい。

   Change the sentences.

2. 文を受動態にしなさい。

   Put the sentences into the passive.

Notes: 2.「直接話法に」into direct speech /「正しい時制に」into the correct tense.
⇒ p.138, p.140 も参照。

d 拡大 — Expansion

((• TRACK 04 09 •))

1. では、繰り返してください。「ジョンは学校に来ます」。

   Now please repeat after me. "John comes to school."

2. 皆さん、文末に yesterday をつけなさい。「ジョンは、昨日学校に来た」。そうです。時制を換えました。

   Add "yesterday" at the end, everyone. "John came to school yesterday." Right. You've changed the tense.

e 短縮 — Contraction

((• TRACK 04 10 •))

1. 短い形で。

   In a short form.

2. その質問で最も重要な部分はどこですか？

   What's the most important part of the question?

3. すべての言葉を繰り返さず答えの部分だけ言いなさい。

   Don't repeat every word. Say only the answering part.

Notes: 文の結合については ⇒ p.141

③ 動作を伴う練習 Practice Using Actions

a TPR — Total Physical Response

((• TRACK 04 11 •))

1. 後ろ［右、左、上、下］を見なさい。

   Look back [right / left / up / down].

2. 右［左］手をあげなさい。

   Raise your right [left] hand.

3.	ひざまずきなさい。	Kneel down.
4.	足を組みなさい。	Cross your legs.
5.	聞いて、そして見なさい。	Listen and look.
6.	膝を曲げなさい。	Bend your knees.
7.	腕を組みなさい。	Fold your arms.
8.	片足で立ちなさい。	Stand on one foot.
9.	片方の手で自分の鼻をさわりなさい。	Touch your nose with one hand.
10.	拡声器を指さしなさい。	Point to the loudspeaker.
11.	2歩前に進みなさい。	Take two steps forward.
12.	両腕を広げなさい。	Stretch your arms out wide.
13.	両手を広げなさい。	Open your hands.
14.	げんこつを作りなさい。	Make a fist.
15.	頭を腕の上に載せなさい。	Rest your head on your arms.
16.	パートナーと握手をしなさい。	Shake hands with your partner.

Notes: TPR（Total Physical Response）では「指示」「命令」を与え、学習者に身体で反応させることによって基本的な表現を理解させる。

b ジャズ・チャンツ　Jazz chants

TRACK 04 12

1.	チャンツを聞きなさい。	Listen to the chant.
2.	リズムに注意しなさい。	Pay attention to the rhythm.
3.	このリズムのパターンを聞きなさい。	Listen to this rhythmic pattern.

4. このリズムとイントネーションのパターンを練習しましょう。 : Let's practice this rhythm and intonation pattern.

5. 安定したビートとリズムを続けてください。 : Keep a steady beat and rhythm, please.

6. いいリズムです。 : That's a good rhythm.

7. そのリズムをそのまま続けなさい。 : Keep up the rhythm.

8. テンポを下げなさい［上げなさい］。 : Slow down [Step up] the tempo.

9. さあ、それを普通のスピードでやってみましょう。 : Now, let's try it at normal speed.

④ 練習の指示 Directions to Practice

a 個人、班ごとの切り替え　Individuals vs. Groups

((• TRACK 04 13 •))

1. 各自でやりなさい。 : Work by yourselves. / Work on your own.

2. 2人で［3人で、4人で］やりなさい。 : Work in pairs [threes / fours].

3. 隣の人と一緒にやりなさい。 : Work with your neighbor.

4. さあ、グループワークをしましょう。 : Now, let's do some group work.

5. グループを作ってください。6人グループです。 : Please form groups. Six students in each group.

6. 小さな円を作りましょう。 : Let's form small circles, shall we?

7. いすを動かして、まっすぐの列を作りなさい。 : Move the chairs and make straight rows.

8.	パートナーを替えましょう。	Let's change partners.

b ノートの取り方・板書の写し方 Note-taking / Copying

((• TRACK 04 14 •))

1.	それらを書き写しなさい。	Write [Copy / Take / Jot] them down.
2.	これらの熟語はとても重要ですから、ノートに書き写しなさい。	These idioms are very important. So copy them into your notebook.

c 図・絵などの説明 Explanation of charts, pictures, etc.

((• TRACK 04 15 •))

1.	15ページの図を見なさい。	Look at the chart on page 15.
2.	これはアメリカのショッピングセンターの絵です。	This is the picture of an American shopping center.

⑤ 書く作業 Writing Activities

a プリントの配布　　Distributing handouts

((• TRACK 04 16 •))

1.	後ろへ回してください。	Pass these (to the) back.
2.	1枚取って後ろへ回してください。	Please take one and pass them back [on].
3.	これらのプリントを配ります。	Let me hand out these copies.

4. 皆さん、練習問題のコピーを持っていますか？	Have you all got a copy of the exercise?
5. プリントを各自で取りなさい。	Help yourselves to the handouts.

生徒の応答 Student Response

プリントをもらえますか？	Could I have a copy? / Can I have a copy?
後ろの席のプリントがありません。	There are no handouts at the back.
あと3枚お願いします。	Three more, please.

b ワークブック　　Workbooks

（TRACK 04 17）

1. ワークブックを出してください。	Take out your workbooks.
2. 12ページを開いて練習問題をしなさい。	Open to page 12 and do the exercises.
3. それぞれの空欄に適語を入れなさい。	Write an appropriate word in each blank.
4. 下の選択肢から句を選び、それぞれの文を完成させなさい。	Complete each sentence with a phrase from the list below.

c OHPで　　By an overhead projector

（TRACK 04 18）

1. OHPでそれをやりましょう。	Let's do it with the OHP.

2.	ここに OHP のシートがあります。	Here is a transparency.
3.	ペンがあるのでこちらへ来て答えを書いてください。	Here's a felt-tip pen [marker]. Come here and write down your answer.
4.	シートに答えを書きなさい。	Write (out) your answers on the transparency.
5.	スクリーンをよく見て。何か見落としています。	Look at the screen carefully. You left something out.
6.	シートに練習問題の答えを書きます。	I'll write down the answers to the exercises on the transparency.
7.	映し出された文をノートに書き写しなさい。	Copy the projected sentences into your notebooks.

生徒の応答 Student Response

スクリーンの下のほうが見えません。	I can't see the bottom of the screen.
スクリーンを少し上げてもらえませんか。	Will you put the screen up a little higher?

d 筆記体・活字体　Handwritten [Script] and block letter style

((TRACK 04 19))

1.	自分の名前を活字体で書きなさい。	Print your name.
		＊活字体で書かせる場合の基本的な指示
2.	自分の名前を大文字の活字体で書きなさい。	Write your name in block letters [block capitals].
3.	筆記体で書きなさい。	Write it in longhand [cursive / script form].
4.	ペンではっきりと活字体で書きなさい。	Print clearly with a pen.

e なぐり書き・丁寧に書く　　Jotting and writing carefully

((• TRACK 04 20 •))

1. きちんと書きなさい。	Write it neatly.
2. 雑に書いたものは受け付けません。	I won't accept messy writing.

f ペン・鉛筆　　Pens and pencils

((• TRACK 04 21 •))

1. 鉛筆［シャープペンシル、ボールペン］で書きなさい。	Write with a pencil [mechanical pencil / ball-point pen].
2. 字が薄すぎます。もっと強く書きなさい。	Your letters are [Your writing is] too light. Press harder.
3. エイチビーの鉛筆［No. 2の鉛筆］を使いなさい。	Use an HB [a hard black] pencil [a Number 2 pencil].
4. 答えを赤いペンでマークしなさい。	Mark your answers with a red pen.

Notes: 3 の Number 2 は HB (= hard black) と同様に鉛筆の芯の硬さを表す。

g 色を塗る　　Coloring

((• TRACK 04 22 •))

1. 色を塗りましょう。	Let's do some coloring [painting].
2. 色鉛筆［クレヨン、パステル］を出しなさい。	Take out your colored pencils [crayons / pastels].
3. 電車を青で塗りなさい。	Color the train blue.
4. 飛行機を描き、それを灰色に塗りなさい。	Draw a plane, and then paint it gray.

h 図を描く — Drawing

((・ TRACK 04 23 ・))

1. 絵を描きましょう。　　　Let's do some drawing.
2. 垂直な線を引きなさい。　Draw a vertical line.
3. 正方形を描きなさい。　　Draw a square.

Notes: 2.「水平な線」horizontal line /「斜線」diagonal line /「曲線」curved line.
3.「丸」circle /「長方形」rectangle /「三角形」triangle /「ひし形」diamond.

⑥ 黒板での作業 At the Board

a チョーク［マーカー］の指示 Using chalk [colored markers]

((・ TRACK 04 24 ・))

1. 白いチョーク［黒いマーカー］を使いなさい。
   Use white chalk [a black marker].

2. 赤ではなく、黄色いチョークを使いなさい。見やすいです。
   Use yellow chalk, not the red one. It's easier to see.

3. 修正のために色の付いたチョーク［マーカー］を使いなさい。
   Use colored chalk [markers] for correcting.

4. チョークが全員分ありますか？
   Are there enough pieces of chalk for everyone?

5. 和男、もっと長いチョークを使いなさい。書きやすいよ。
   Use a longer piece of chalk, Kazuo. It's easier to write with.

6. 違う色のチョーク［マーカー］で絵を描きなさい。
   Draw your picture with the different colored chalk [markers].

b 板書の指示 — What and where to write

((• TRACK 04 25 •))

1. （そこではなく）ここに書きなさい。 — Write here (not there).
2. 黒板の下のほうを使ってはいけません。 — Don't use the lower part of the blackboard.
3. 黒板の中央に書きなさい。 — Write in the middle of the blackboard.
4. 後ろの黒板も使っていいです。 — You may use the board at the back of the room, too.
5. 各自の場所にきちんと答えを書きなさい。 — Write your answers neatly in each block.
6. 上から下の順で文を書きなさい。 — Write your sentences in order from top to bottom.

Notes: 5 は教師が書く場所を仕切っておいた場合の指示。

生徒の応答 Student Response

文字が見えません。	I can't see those letters.
もっと大きな字で書いてください。	Please write in much larger letters.
もっとはっきり書いてください。	Write it more clearly.

c 下線を引く — Underlining

((• TRACK 04 26 •))

1. その語［文］に下線を引いてください。 — Please underline the word [the sentence].

2. 下線を引いた語を見て。1つ間違いがあります。 | Look at the underlined word. There is a mistake in it.

3. 2つの重要な単語に下線を引きました。声に出して読みなさい。 | I've underlined two important words. Read them aloud.

4. 太郎が黒板に書いた答えには間違いが2つあります。そこに下線を引きます。 | Taro's answer on the board has two mistakes. I'll underline them.

5. 最も重要な語に二重の下線を引きなさい。 | Draw a double line under the most important word.

d 板書を消す — Cleaning the board

TRACK 04 27

1. これらを消してもいいですか？ | May I erase these?

2. 黒板のこちら側を消していいかな？ | Is it all right to erase this side of the board?

3. では、それをすぐに写しなさい。最初の部分を消したいので。 | Now, copy it quickly. I want to erase the first part.

Notes: 黒板の掃除に関する一般的指示は⇒ p.61

Classroom English Handbook

Chapter 5 教科書本文

Main Text

① 読み方 Reading

a 範読 — Model reading

((• TRACK 04 28 •))

1. では CD の聞き取り練習をしましょう。	Now, we'll do a CD-listening exercise.
2. 新出単語を CD で聞きなさい。	Listen to the CD for new words.
3. 新出単語の読み方を教えます。	I'll show you how to read the new words.
4. CD を聞いて、本文の読み方を確認します。	We'll listen to the CD to see how to read this text.
5. まず私が本文を読みます。	First, I'll read the text for you.
6. スーザンにテキストを読んでもらいます。 ＊ ALT か音読の上手な生徒に範読してもらう場合	I'd like Suzan to read the text for the class.

b 教師のあとについて読む — Reading after the teacher

((• TRACK 04 29 •))

1. 繰り返してください。	Repeat [Read] after me.
2. では本文を音読しましょう。私に続けて読んでください。	Now let's read the text aloud. You'll follow along as I read it.

III 授業展開

3. 私の口をよく見て、同じように口を動かしなさい。 : Watch my mouth and move your mouth as I do.

生徒の応答 Student Response

よく聞こえません。	Excuse me, I cannot hear you well.
もう少し大きな声でお願いします。	Read more loudly, please.
読み方を教えてください。	Show me how to read it, please.
もっとゆっくり読んでください。	Please read more slowly.

C CDのあとについて読む　Reading after the CD

TRACK 04 30

1. CDを聞いて繰り返しなさい。 : (Please) listen and repeat after the CD.
2. 読む準備はいいですか。では、CDを流します。 : Are you ready to read? OK. I'll start the CD.
3. これはCDのあとから読む練習です。 : This is a practice in reading after the CD.

生徒の応答 Student Response

音量を上げて［下げて］ください。	(Excuse me,) could you turn up [down] the volume?
もう一度聞きたいです。	I'd like to hear it once more.
CDを止める回数をもっと多くしてください。	Stop the CD more often.

d 音読 — Oral reading

TRACK 04 31

1.	では、音読を始めましょう。	Now, let's start oral reading [reading aloud].
2.	本文を音読します。	Let's read the text aloud.
3.	感情を込めて音読しなさい。	Read the text aloud with feeling.
4.	音読するのを聞かせてください。用意はいいですか？	Let me hear you read the text aloud. Are you ready?
5.	よく聞こえません。大きな声で読みなさい。	I cannot hear you well. Read in a big [loud] voice.
6.	読み方がはっきりしていません。もっとはっきり読みなさい。	Your reading is not clear enough. Read more clearly.
7.	どのくらい自然に音読できるか見てみましょう。 ＊内容に合った読み方ができるか確認する場合	Let's see how naturally we can read the text aloud.

e 黙読 — Silent reading

TRACK 04 32

1.	では、黙読をしてみましょう。	Now, let's try silent reading. / And now it's time for silent reading. / Please read the text silently.
2.	CDを聞いて、それに合わせて本文を黙読します。	Listening to and following the CD, we'll read the text silently.
3.	まず本文を黙読し、それから音読をします。	First, we'll read the text silently and then we'll read it aloud.

4.	もう一度本文を読みますが、今度は黙読です。	We will read the text again. But this time we'll do silent reading.
5.	音読はしません。今回は同じ部分を黙読します。	No more oral reading. This time we will read the same part silently.

Notes: 生徒に黙読をさせる際の指示を紹介した。2はCDのスピードに合わせての黙読の指示。

🔊 個人読み　　　　　　　　　　　　　Individual reading

ア．みんなに向けて読む場合　Reading for the class　(((• TRACK 04 33 •)))

1.	由香里、本文を音読してくれますか？	Yukari, will you read (the text) aloud (for the class)?
2.	誰か本文を読んでくれますか？	Any volunteers to read the text? / Would anyone like to volunteer to read the text?
3.	では、恵と悠一はこの段落を皆さんに向けて読みなさい。	Now Megumi and Yuichi will read this paragraph to the class.
4.	恵は最初の3文を、悠一は最後の4文を読んでください。	Megumi, you'll read the first three sentences, and Yuichi the last four sentences.

イ．生徒が各自で読む場合　Buzz reading　(((• TRACK 04 34 •)))

1.	では、各自で読みましょう。	Now, (let's try) individual reading.
2.	クラスで一斉に読む必要はありません。	You don't have to read in chorus.
3.	ゆっくり読んでも、速くても構いません。	You may read slowly or you may read fast.

Notes: 机間巡視で生徒がしっかり読んでいるかを確認し、個々の生徒の音読の問題点を指導するようにしたい。

g ペア読み　　Pair reading

((• TRACK 04 35 •))

1. ペア読みをしましょう。	Let's do pair reading. / Let's practice reading in pairs. / Now we'll do pair reading.
2. 一人が声を出して読み、もう一人はそれを聞きましょう。	One of you will read aloud and the other will listen (to him or her).
3. 一人が読んで、もう一人は聞いたことをすべて書き取りなさい。	One of you will read as the other listens and writes whatever he or she hears.

h 斉読　　Choral reading

((• TRACK 04 36 •))

1. 本文をみんなで一緒に読みましょう。	Let's read the text all together.
2. 声をそろえて読みましょう。	Let's begin choral reading. / Let's read in chorus.
3. さあ、みんなで私のあと［CD］について読みましょう。	Now, all of you will read after me [after the CD].

❶ 読む箇所の指定 — Directions about where to read

(((• TRACK 04 37 •)))

1. 31ページの5行目です。 — Page 31, line 5.
2. 7課のセクション2から始めましょう。 — We will begin at Lesson 7, Section 2.
3. 22, 23ページの下にある新出単語を読む練習をしましょう。 — We will practice reading the new words at the bottom of pages 22 and 23.
4. 最初の段落の2番目の文を読みましょう。 — Let's read the second sentence of the first paragraph [sentence 2 of paragraph 1].
5. 58頁の最初の1行目から（同じ頁の5行目まで）読んでください。 — Will you read from the first line [line 1] on page 58 (to line 5 on the same page)?

生徒の応答 Student Response

どのページ（のどの行）ですか？	What page (and what line)?
どこからどこまでですか？	Where should I start and where should I stop?

❷ イントネーション — Intonation

(((• TRACK 04 38 •)))

1. イントネーションをしっかりつけて。 — With good intonation.
2. イントネーションに注意しなさい。 — Be careful about the intonation.
3. 上昇する［下降する］イントネーションで文を終わりなさい。こんなふうに。 — End the sentence with a rising [falling] intonation. Like this.

k 強勢　　Stress / Accent

((• TRACK 04 39 •))

1. calendar の強勢は len ではなく、ca にあります。　　The (strong) stress of 'calendar' is on 'ca', not on 'len'.
2. 正しい強勢で語を読みなさい。　　Read the word with the correct stress.
3. この語の強勢に注意しなさい。　　Be careful about the stress of this word.
4. この語の正しい強勢を教えましょう。　　I'll give you the correct stress of this word.
5. 間違った節に強勢を置いています。　　You put a stress on the wrong syllable.

Notes: イントネーション、強勢については p.113 も参照。

l 発音の訂正　　Correcting mistakes in pronunciation

((• TRACK 04 40 •))

1. 発音[アクセント、イントネーション]が適切ではありません。　　That's not a good pronunciation [accent / intonation].
2. 読みにいくつか間違いがありました。　　There were a few [a couple of] mistakes in your reading.
3. あなたの読み方を訂正しましょう。　　Let me correct your reading.
4. CD のように読んでみるといいですよ。　　You should try to read it more like the CD.
5. もっと上手に読めると思いますよ。　　I'm sure you can read much better.

6. ちょっと待って、洋介。それは /fáinəli/ であって、/fínəli/ ではない。
   * finally の発音を訂正する場合の例

   Just a moment, Yosuke. That should be /fáinəli/, not /fínəli/.

7. 君の busy という語の発音は正しくないです。正しくは /bízi/ です。

   Your pronunciation of the word 'busy' is not correct. The correct one is /bízi/.

生徒の応答 Student Response

どこが悪いのですか？	Tell me what's wrong with my reading.
英語で b-u-s-y を何と発音しますか？	How do you say b-u-s-y in English?
この語の発音の仕方を教えてください。	Please tell me the pronunciation of this word.

② 内容把握 Comprehension

a 語[句・文]の意味　Meaning of words [phrases / sentences]

TRACK 04 41

1. この語の意味は何ですか？

   What does this word mean? / What is the meaning of this word?

2. 日本語でこの語［句］の意味を言ってください。

   Tell me the meaning of this word [phrase] in Japanese.

3. 辞書には何と載っていましたか？

   What does your dictionary say?

b 段落の大意　　　　　　　　　　　　Gist of paragraph

ア．大意把握の指示　Summarizing　　　TRACK 04 42

1. 段落を要約しましょう。　　　　Let's summarize the paragraph.
2. この段落の大意は何ですか？　　What's a summary of this paragraph? / What does this paragraph say in short?
3. 自分の言葉でそれを言い直せますか？　Can you restate that in your own words?

イ．大意把握の具体的方法　Skimming and scanning　　　TRACK 04 43

1. （もし要約するとしたら）この段落にはどんなタイトルが考えられますか？　　What title can you think of for this paragraph (if you summarize it)?
2. この段落の鍵となる語を見つけなさい。　　Take out the key word [words] in this paragraph.
3. 鍵となる語を使って、その段落の簡単な要約をしなさい。　　Make a short summary of the paragraph, using the key word [words].
4. その段落の大意を最もよく表している文はどれですか？　　Which sentence summarizes the paragraph best?
5. この段落の主題文はどれですか？　　Which is the topic sentence of this paragraph?
6. この段落には主題文がないようです。　　This paragraph seems to have no topic sentence.

c 指示語の把握 — Understanding determiners

((TRACK 04 44))

1. この it は A ですか B ですか？
   Is this 'it' A or B?

2. この them は何を表していますか？
   What is this 'them'?

3. these が指すものを言ってください。
   Tell me what 'these' refers to.

4. この he は誰を指していますか。本文から探して言いなさい。
   Who does this 'he' refer to? Find and tell me who he is from the text.

5. (7行目の) they は本文中で何を表していますか？
   What does this 'they' (on line 7) stand for in the text?

d 和訳 — Translation

ア．和訳の指示 Directions

((TRACK 04 45))

1. 日本語でお願いします。
   In Japanese, please.

2. この文を日本語に訳してください。
   Put this sentence into Japanese. / Will you translate this sentence into Japanese?

3. さあ皆さん。それを日本語に訳せるかどうか見てみましょう。
   Now class, let's see if we can translate it into Japanese.

イ．和訳をよくしようとする場合 Improving students' translation

((TRACK 04 46))

1. もっとうまく訳すことができますよ。もう一度やってみなさい。
   You can make your translation better. Try it again.

2. 一語一語厳密に和訳するよりも、英文の意味を自然な日本語に訳したほうがいいです。 ／ It's better to translate the meaning of English sentences into natural Japanese than to translate each word exactly.

3. もっと口語表現を使った和訳は考えられませんか。今度はふつうの日本語を使ってください。 ／ Can't you think of a more colloquial translation? This time use everyday Japanese.

4. あなたの和訳は、意味はわかりますが変です。もっとわかりやすくする方法を考えなさい。 ／ Your translation sounds strange, though it is understandable. Think about how you can improve it [make it better].

生徒の応答 Student Response

| 辞書を引いてもいいですか？ | Can I use the dictionary? / Is it OK if I use a dictionary? |

e パラフレーズ　Paraphrasing

1. この表現［文］をほかの言葉で言い換えなさい。 ／ Paraphrase this expression [sentence].

2. この句の意味を別のやさしい英語で言いなさい。 ／ Tell me the meaning of this phrase in different but easy English.

3. この語［句］と同じ意味の語［句］を本文から見つけなさい。 ／ Find a word [a phrase] in the text which has almost the same meaning as this word [phrase].

4. この語は実際にはどんなことを表していますか。日本語でも英語でもいいので自分の言葉で言ってみてください。 ／ What idea does this word really express? Tell me in your own words, either in Japanese or in English.

③ 文法練習 Grammar Drills

ａ 書き換え　　　　　　　　　　　　　　Rewriting

((• TRACK 04 48 •))

1. どのように書き換えますか？ — How do you rewrite it?

2. 次の文を書き換えなさい。 — Rewrite the following sentence(s).

3. the girl で始めて文の形を代えなさい。 — Change the sentence form by starting with "the girl."

4. 副詞節をすべて副詞句に直して書き換えなさい。 — Change all the adverbial clauses into adverbial phrases.

5. 違う構文を使って同じ意味を表しなさい。 — Use a different sentence structure to express the same meaning.

6. He plays tennis very well. という文を a tennis player という語を使って書き換えなさい。 — Rewrite the sentence "He plays tennis very well." using the words "a tennis player."

Notes: p.116, p.140 も参照。

ｂ 和文英訳　　　　　　　　　　　　Putting Japanese into English

ア．和文英訳の指示 Directions

((• TRACK 04 49 •))

1. では英訳をしてみましょう。 — Now (let's try) English translation.

2. 英語に訳してみましょう。 — Let's try translating it into English.

3. 日本語の文を英語に訳してください。 — Put the Japanese sentence(s) into English.

Chapter 5 | 教科書本文

4. それぞれの日本語の文の意味を英語で言ってみましょう。	Let's say in English the meaning of each Japanese sentence.

イ．誤りを訂正する場合 Correcting mistakes　　((• TRACK 04 50 •))

1. 間違いはありませんか？	No errors [mistakes]? / (Have you found) any mistakes? / Are there any mistakes [errors]?
2. うっかりミス［スペルミス］に気づきましたか？	(Have you found) any careless [spelling] mistakes?
3. （この訳は）修正が必要ではないですか？	(Doesn't this translation need) any correction?
4. （この訳には）何か問題がありますか？	(Does this translation have) any problems?

Notes: 英訳の訂正は教師が一方的に行うのでなく、生徒に間違いに気づかせ、できれば自分で訂正させるように指導したい。

ウ．別の訳を検討する場合 Alternative translation　　((• TRACK 04 51 •))

1. 違う訳がありますか？	Is there a different translation?
2. これを訳す別の方法はありますか？	(Do you have) another way of translating this?
3. 違う訳し方をした人は手を挙げてください。	Raise your hand if you translated it differently.

C 穴埋め　　Completion

((• TRACK 04 52 •))

1. どの語がここに来ますか？	What word comes here? / What word should go here?
2. 空欄を埋めなさい。	Fill in the blanks [the gaps].

Ⅲ
授業展開

3. 空欄に適語を入れなさい。	Put the right words into the blanks.
4. 下から適語を選んで、空欄を埋めなさい。	Fill in each blank with the right word from below. / For each blank choose the most suitable [fitting] word from below.
5. 下の選択肢から適切な副詞を選んで、それぞれの文に挿入しなさい。	Insert into each sentence a suitable adverb from the list below.

d 文の転換・結合　Conversion and combination

ア．文の転換 Conversion

((TRACK 04 53))

1. 文を否定形に［疑問形に］直しなさい。	Turn the sentences into negative forms [question forms].
2. それぞれの文の態を換えなさい。	Change the voice of each sentence.
3. それを物語文に換えなさい。	Change it into the narrative form.
4. かっこの中の動詞を未来形に換えなさい。	Put the verbs in brackets into the future tense.
5. 引用符で囲まれた文を that, what, if などを使って書き換えなさい。	Change the sentences in quotation marks, using that, what, if, etc.

Notes: 1「感嘆文に」into exclamatory sentences /「命令文に」into imperative sentences /「平叙文に」into declarative sentences.
文法用語を避けるとしたら5のように例を挙げて指示をすることになる。p.116, 138 も参照。

イ．文の結合 Combination

(((・ TRACK 04 54 ・)))

1. 適切な関係代名詞をそれぞれのかっこに入れなさい。

   Fill in each bracket with a suitable relative pronoun.

2. which, who, that などを使って2つの文を1つにしなさい。

   Put the two sentences together, using such words as *which, who, that,* etc.

3. but, because, though などを使って2つの文を1つにしなさい。

   Put the two sentences together, using words like *but, because, though,* etc.

4. where, when, how などを使って2つの文を結びつけなさい。

   Connect the two sentences with words like *where, when, how,* etc.

④ 言語活動 Performance Activities

a 聞くこと　　　　　　　　　　　Listening

(((・ TRACK 04 55 ・)))

1. 2人の旧友の挨拶を聞きなさい。

   Listen to the greeting between two old friends.

2. CDをもう一度聞いて、答えを確認しなさい。

   Check your answers by listening to the CD again.

3. インタビューの内容を聞く前に、質問を見なさい。

   Look at these questions before listening to the interview.

4. ビンゴゲームの説明を聞き、説明にしたがってパートナーと一緒にやりましょう。

   Listen to the instructions for a Bingo game and follow them with your partner.

b 話すこと　　Speaking

TRACK 04 56

1. 繰り返して。私はリンゴが好きです。　　Repeat after me; I like apples.

   (生徒：I like apples.)

   オレンジ。　　Oranges.

   (生徒：I like oranges.)

   ヘビ。　　Snakes.

   (生徒：I like snakes.)

2. どんな果物が好きですか、美恵子？　　What fruit do you like, Mieko?

   (生徒：Strawberries.)

   さあ、皆さん。美恵子はイチゴが好きです。　　Now everyone; Mieko likes strawberries.

   (生徒：Mieko likes strawberries.)

   祐二はどうですか？　　How about you, Yuji?

3. 私の手にあるこれは何ですか？　＊カップを持って　　What is this in my hand?

   そうです。私は手にカップを持っています。　　Yes, I have a cup in my hand.

   皆さん、繰り返して。「あなたは手にカップを持っています」。　　Repeat after me, everyone; you have a cup in your hand.

   さあ、私は手に何を持っていますか？　　＊スプーンを手にして　　Now, what do I have in my hand?

   はい、私は手にスプーンを持っています。　　Yes, I have a spoon in my hand.

c 読むこと — Reading

(((• TRACK 04 57 •)))

1. その話［一節］を読んで質問に答えなさい。 : Read the story [the passage] and answer the questions about it.
2. これから読む話にしたがって絵を描きなさい。 : Draw a picture according to the story you are going to read.
3. 左側の英単語に合う日本語の単語を右から見つけなさい。 : Match the English words on the left with the Japanese words on the right.
4. 左側と右側の単語のグループを組み合わせて文を作りなさい。 : Match the groups of words on the left and the right to make sentences.

d 書くこと — Writing

(((• TRACK 04 58 •)))

1. この書式に記入しなさい。 : Fill in this form.
2. 出席番号と名前を書きなさい。 : Write your number and name.
3. 英語で日曜日の日記をつけなさい。 : Write your Sunday diary in English.
4. 単語の綴りを言います。聞き取ってノートに単語を書きなさい。 : I'll give you spellings of words. Listen and write down each word in your notebook(s).

Chapter 6 終了

Consolidation

① 残り時間 Remaining Time

a 残り時間が短い場合 — Little time left

ア．急いで進む In a hurry   (TRACK 04 59)

1.	12時まであと7分です。	It's seven (minutes) to twelve now.
2.	そろそろ昼休みの時間です。	It's almost lunch time [time for the lunch break].
3.	たった2, 3分しかありません。	Only a few minutes to go [spare]. / We have only a few minutes to go [spare].
4.	もう時間がありません。	We're running out of time.
5.	急ぎましょう。	Let's hurry up.
6.	これをするのにあと10分しかありません。	You have ten minutes to do this.
7.	急いで練習問題Dを終えましょう。	Let's hurry up and finish Exercise D.
8.	最後のものをやってしまいましょう。	Let's get the last thing done.
9.	ほとんど時間がありません。	There's almost no time (left).
10.	チャイムが鳴るところです。	The bell is going to ring in a moment.

Notes: 1〜6までのいずれかの表現だけでも状況によっては急いで作業を進めるように促す意味になる。7, 8などを付け加えると意図がより明確に伝わるようになる。1, 2では各校の時間割により、授業終了時間の少し前の時刻を代入して使う。9, 10では、時間がないから本日はこのあたりで終了するという意味になる。

生徒の応答 Student Response

終わりにしましょう。	Let's stop now. / Let's finish.
はあ、疲れました。	We're tired. Whew!
帰ろう。	Let's go home.

イ．生徒を呼び止めて Asking students to wait   (TRACK 04 60)

1. 待ってください。 — (Please) wait. / Just a moment, please. / Wait a moment.
2. 急いではいけません。 — Don't go rushing off.
3. 席に座っていなさい。 — (Please) stay in your seats.
4. 行く前にもう一つやることがあります。 — One more thing before you go.
5. だめです。チャイムはまだ鳴っていません。 — No, no, no. The bell hasn't rung yet.
6. まだ終わる時間ではありません。 — It isn't time to finish yet.
7. 席に戻りなさい。 — Go back to your places [seats].
8. 静かに座っていなさい。他のクラスはまだ授業中です。 — Sit quietly. The other classes are still working.

ⓑ 残り時間が長い場合   Much time left

ア．予定外の活動を入れる Using the final minutes of class   (TRACK 04 61)

1. 12時まで10分だけあります。 — It's only ten to twelve.
2. チャイムはまだ鳴っていません。 — The bell hasn't rung yet.

3.	授業の終わりまで2, 3分あります。質問はありますか？	We have a few more minutes to go. Any questions?
4.	ずいぶん早く終わりましたね。	You finished that quickly.
5.	もう1つ活動をしましょう。	Let's do an extra activity.
6.	ゲームをするのはどう？	What do you say to playing a game?
7.	25ページの図をざっと見ましょう。	Let's have a quick look at the chart on page 25.

Notes: 1〜4に5〜7を付け加えると、余った時間で予定外の活動を行う旨を述べることができる。

イ．早めに終わる Finishing earlier than planned

(((• TRACK 04 62 •)))

1.	今もう終わりますか？	Can we finish now?
2.	すごい！ いつもより早く問題が終わりました。	Great! You finished your tasks earlier than usual.
3.	静かに退出しなさい。	Go out quietly (, please).
4.	静かに！ ほかのクラスは授業中です。	Ssshhhhh! Other classes are still working.

Notes: 3と4は他のクラスへの配慮を伝える表現である。

C 予定の変更　　　　　　　　　　　Change of schedule

(((• TRACK 04 63 •)))

1.	この活動は次回にしましょう。	Let's do this activity next time.

2. 家で練習問題 B を終わらせてください。 : Please finish Exercise B at home.

3. それは次回に回しましょう。 : Let's put it off till next time.

4. 練習問題 D を残しておきましょう。 : Let's leave out Exercise D.

5. 45 ページは抜かしませんか？ : Why don't we skip page 45?

6. 今日は小テストはしません。 : I'm not going to give a quiz today.

Notes:「予定外の活動を入れる」p. 145 も参照。

d 次回の予告　Announcement for the next class

((TRACK 04 64))

1. 来週の授業には辞書 [CD] を持ってきてください。 : Please bring your dictionary [CD] next week to class.

2. 次回、（必ず）自分の写真を持ってきなさい。 : (Do) bring your photograph next time.

3. 次回は読書記録を忘れないように。 : Don't forget your reading record next time.

4. ファイルを忘れずに持ってきて。来週使います。 : Don't forget your files [folders]. We need them next week.

Notes: 4 は来週必ず持って来てほしいということ。

e チャイム　　　　　　　　　　　　　　　　　Bell

((• TRACK 04 65 •))

1.	あー、チャイムだ！	Oh, no! The bell!
2.	終わりの時間です。	It's time to stop now.
3.	今日はここまでです。	That's all for today. ＊最も一般的な表現
		Let's call it a day. / Well, that's it.
4.	解散！	Class dismissed. / You can go now.
5.	時間がきました。	Time is up.

Notes: 4は日本の教科書ではなじみがうすいが、英米では一般的な表現である。ただし、教師側の権威を感じさせる表現なので使えるのは小学校、中学校まで。5は時間内に終わらせるように言っておいた作業やゲームなどの最中にも使える。

② 宿題の指示 Homework / Assignment

a 教科書の該当箇所　　　　　　　　　Where in the text

ア．宿題の指示 Directions for homework

((• TRACK 04 66 •))

1.	14頁は宿題です。	Page 14. This is [It's] your homework.
2.	15頁を開いてください。練習問題A, C, Dは宿題です。	Turn (back) to page 15. Exercises A, C, and D are your homework.
3.	16頁を開いてください。10行目から23行目は宿題です。	Open your books to page 16. From line 10 to line 23 is your homework.
4.	家で34頁の初めの会話を読んできなさい。	Read the introductory conversation on page 34 at home.
5.	13, 14頁の重要な文を家で復習しなさい。	Review the key sentences on pages 13 and 14 at home.

6.	このページの上の［下の］半分が今日の［次回までの］宿題です。	The upper [lower] half of this page is your homework for today [next time].
7.	家で図［表、会話］を完成させなさい。	Complete the chart [list / dialog] at home.
8.	今日は練習問題の一部だけをやりました。家で全部やってきなさい。	We have done only part of the exercises today. Finish them off at home.

イ．指示の確認 Are the directions clear?

((• TRACK 04 67 •))

1.	わかりますか？	Is it clear? / Do you get it [understand]? / Did you follow that [me]? / Can you follow this?
2.	質問がありますか？	Any questions?
3.	いいですか？ ＊ informal な表現	Okay? / Right? / All right? / Got it? / Are you with me?

b 暗唱文の指定　　For recitation

((• TRACK 04 68 •))

1.	この表現を暗記しなさい。	Learn these expressions by heart.
2.	7番は暗記しなくていいです。	(You can) leave out No. 7.
3.	四角で囲った表現を覚えなさい。	You should memorize the expressions in the box.

c 単語・句の確認　　Checking the new words and phrases

ア．予 習 Preparation

((• TRACK 04 69 •))

1.	予習しなければなりません。	Preparation is a must. ＊must＝（口語）「絶対に必要なもの」

2.	新出単語は辞書で調べてください。	Look up the new words in your dictionary.
3.	単語帳を用意して新出単語はすべてそこに書きなさい。	Prepare a word book and put every new word in it. ＊word book＝「単語帳」
4.	教科書の後ろで語彙を確かめることができます。	You can check the vocabulary at the back of the textbook.
5.	文脈から意味を推測しなさい。	Try to guess the meaning from the context.

Notes: 5は多読・速読などで辞書を引きすぎないよう指導をする時の表現。

イ. 練習 Practice

(((• TRACK 04 70 •)))

1.	家で新出単語を練習しなさい。	Practice the new words at home.
2.	単語リストに目を通して、ノートに新出単語を書きなさい。	Go through the word list and write the new words in your notebook.
3.	これらの語を正確に書けるようにしなさい。	Learn to spell these words correctly.

d プリント　　　　　　　　　　　　Handout

(((• TRACK 04 71 •)))

1.	これが、本日［明日、次回］のプリントです。	These are the handouts for today [tomorrow / next time].
2.	帰る前に1枚取って行ってください。	Take one as you leave. / Pick up one sheet before you go.

Notes:「プリントの配布」は⇒ p.120

e 小テストの予告 — Announcement of a quiz

1. 来週、小テストがあります。
   There will be a quiz next week.
2. 次回の授業でディクテーションをします。
   I'm going to give a dictation in the next lesson.
3. 次の月曜日にテストがあることを忘れないように。
   Don't forget that you are taking a test next Monday.
4. 次の金曜日に5課の小テストをします。
   I'll give you a quiz on Lesson 5 this coming Friday.

③ 終わりの挨拶 Closing Remarks

a 一般的な挨拶 — Departing

1. 皆さん、さようなら。
   Good-bye, class [everybody / everyone].
2. また明日。
   See you tomorrow. / I'll see you tomorrow. / Good-bye till tomorrow.
3. じゃあね、健。
   ＊informalな表現
   Bye now, Ken.
4. 気をつけてね。
   ＊家へ帰る生徒に
   Take care.

生徒の応答 Student Response

トムソン先生、さようなら。	Good-bye, Ms. [Mr.] Thompson.
はい、ありがとうございます。　＊Take care.と言われて	Yes (, I will). Thank you.

b 来週まで　　　　　　　　　　　　　　　　　Until next week

(((・ TRACK 04 74 ・)))

1. また来週。
   See you next week. / Good-bye and see you next week. / I'll see you next week.

2. 良い週末を。
   Have a nice weekend. / Enjoy your weekend.

c 次時まで間が空く場合　　When the next class is far ahead

(((・ TRACK 04 75 ・)))

1. 来月また会いましょう。
   I won't see you until next month.

2. 次に会うのは再来週ですから、宿題を終えておきなさい。
   I won't see you next week. So, make sure your assignment is finished.

3. 宿題を忘れないように。
   Don't forget your assignment.

4. 毎日英語を勉強しなさい［CDを聞きなさい］。
   (Please) try to study English [listen to the CD] every day.

5. 休みを楽しんでね。けど次回の授業の準備を忘れないこと。
   Enjoy the break. But be sure you're ready for the next class.

d 長期休暇の前　　　　　　　　　　　　Before a (long) vacation

(((・ TRACK 04 76 ・)))

1. 9月に会いましょう。
   See you in September.

2. 皆さんに会うのは冬休み［クリスマス休暇］明けです。
   I'll see you all again after the Christmas holidays [vacation].
   ＊ Christmas holidays を使うのはイギリス英語、Christmas vacation を使うのはアメリカ英語

3. 休暇を楽しんでください。
   Have a nice [good] vacation. / Enjoy your vacation.

Chapter 6 | 終　了

e 時間割変更の予告　　Change of schedule announcement

((• TRACK 04 77 •))

1. 次週から、授業は8時40分に始まります。
   ＊夏時間（summer time）の時
   　School starts at 8:40 from next week.

2. 次週は短縮時間になります。
   　We'll have shorter periods next week.

3. 授業は正午に終わります。
   　School will be over at noon.

4. 1時限は40分となります。
   　One period will be 40 minutes.

5. 休み時間は5分に短縮されます。
   　Break time will be reduced [shortened] to five minutes.

6. 月曜から金曜まで午後の授業はありません。
   　All the afternoon classes will be cancelled from Monday through Friday.

f 休講の予告　　Announcement of lecture [class] cancellation

((• TRACK 04 78 •))

1. 明日は授業はありません。
   　No class tomorrow. / We have no class tomorrow. / There's no lesson tomorrow.

2. 出張です。
   　I'm going on a business trip. / I have to make [go on] an official trip. / I'm scheduled to go on a business trip.

3. 東京で会議があります。
   　I have to attend a meeting in Tokyo.

4. 明日は東京の学校を訪問します。
   　I'm visiting a school in Tokyo tomorrow.

5. 教員の会議に出ます。
   　I have to attend a teachers' conference.

6. 明日はスポーツ大会の練習です。
   　We will have practice for Sports Day tomorrow.

Ⅲ　授業展開

Notes: 「出張」に相当する便利な英単語はない。生徒に用件まで言う必要がない時には I'll be out of town. のような言い方で十分であろう。

g あと片づけ　　Clearing the classroom

(((• TRACK 04 79 •)))

1. 黒板をきれいにしてください。	**Clean the board, will you?**
2. エアコンを切ってください。	**Switch off the air-conditioner, will you?**
3. 電気を切ってください。	**Turn off the lights, will you?**
4. ブースの中の主電源を切ってください。 ＊LL教室で	**(Please) turn [switch] off the main switches in your booths.**
5. 帰る前に、机といすを元通りにしなさい。	**Tidy up your desks and chairs before you go.**
6. （持ち物を）すべて持ちましたか？	**Have you got everything [your things]?**

Notes: 6は移動教室などで忘れ物がないかどうか確認する表現。日本語で言う「忘れ物はありませんか」。

生徒の応答 Student Response

（先生の注意に対して）はい、わかりました。	Yes, sir, I will. / Sure. / OK. / Why not? / No problem.

Classroom English Handbook

小中連携のための
ヒント

**Hints for Cooperation between
Elementary and Junior High Schools**

「教室英語」は、簡潔に定義すれば「授業の中で用いられる英語」である。しかし実際には、非常に多様な表現で成り立っている。授業では認知、技能、情意の領域に関する様々なやりとり（interactions）があるからである。授業では人間（教師）が人間（生徒）を相手にして、説明、質疑応答を行う。その中では喜怒哀楽の様々な場面が出てくる。教室英語はそれらを対象にして、授業に活気を与えたり、生徒の心を推し量りながら用いられる。「先生のあの一言」によって生徒が生き返ることもあれば、時には「死」に至ることもある。

　つまり、教室英語は単なる例文集ではない。授業でどのように生かして使うかによって、授業にも生徒にも活気を与えることができるものである。そのためには、例文を暗記するだけでなく、授業の流れと一体化させる必要がある。この「小中連携のためのヒント」では、指導例を出しながら、どのように教室英語を用いるのかを説明している。それは「英語で英語を教える」ことの実践例となっている。

Chapter 1 オーラル・コミュニケーション
Oral Communication

a 日常会話 Daily conversation

ア．授業前にリラックスさせる Let's relax (((• TRACK 05 01 •)))

1. さあ、みんなリラックスして。 / Now, class, please relax.
2. 真紀さん、落ち着いて。 / Take it easy, Maki.
3. 緊張していますね。リラックスして。 / You look nervous. Just relax.
4. リラックスして大きな声で話しましょう、いい？ / Let's relax a little, and speak up, OK?
5. 皆さん、大きく深呼吸してみましょう。 / Everybody, take a deep breath.
6. 授業を始める前にみんなで歌ってリラックスしましょう。 / Before starting the lesson, let's sing together to relax a little bit.

Notes: オーラル・コミュニケーションの授業は、スピーキングが中心で生徒が過度に緊張しやすい。授業の導入時に緊張をほぐさせることを念頭に、リラックスさせるための例文を示した。

イ．自分のことを話させる Talk about oneself (((• TRACK 05 02 •)))

1. さあ、クラスの皆に自分のことを話しましょう。 / Now please tell the class about yourself.
2. 3文で自分のことを話してください。 / Please tell (us) about yourself in three sentences.

3.	昨日は放課後何をしましたか？ 話してください。	What did you do yesterday after school? Please tell us.
4.	昨日は日曜日です。どこかへ行きましたか。クラスの皆に話してください。	Yesterday was Sunday. Did you go anywhere? Please tell the class.
5.	夏休みの予定は何ですか？ 話してください。	What are your plans for summer vacation? Please tell us.

Notes: 1, 2 の一般的指示は具体的な発話の場面を想定していることが普通である。3 以下は生徒が自己表現できるように、身近なことを語る機会を想定し、そのための発問を例示している。

ウ．ペアで活動させる　Pair activity

(((TRACK 05 03)))

1.	次の活動はペアで行いなさい。	Please do the next activity in pairs.
2.	ペアになってあらかじめ考えた５つの質問を相手に聞きましょう。	Please pair off [up] and ask your partner the five questions you have prepared.
3.	ペアになって昨日したことをお互いに聞きましょう。	Please pair off [up] and ask each other what you did yesterday.
4.	ペアになって相手とノートを交換しなさい。そこにお互いのコメントを書いてください。	Please pair off [up] and exchange your notebooks with your partners and write down each other's comments.
5.	前後の生徒とペアになりなさい。そして会話文を音読する練習をしなさい。	Make a pair with the student behind or in front of you. Then please practice reading the dialog aloud.

Chapter 1 | オーラル・コミュニケーション

6. ペアになって私が出した問題を解きなさい。最後に、1つの組にクラスのみんなに報告してもらいます。	Please pair off [up] and solve the questions I have given you. At the end, I'll ask one of the pairs to report to the class.

エ．グループで活動させる Group activity   (((• TRACK 05 04 •)))

1. 3人組［4人組、5人組］を作りスキットの練習をしてください。	Please make groups of three [four / five] and practice the skit.
2. 4人1組になり、スキットを演じる練習をしなさい。	Form groups of four and practice acting out the skit.
3. 3人1組になり、短いスキットを書いてください。完成したら持ってきてください。	Form groups of three and write a short skit. When you have finished, please bring it to me.
4. 4人1組になり、2人ずつ向き合うように机を動かしなさい。そして、一緒に発音の練習をしましょう。	Get into groups of four and arrange the desks so two people can face the other two and practice pronunciation together.

Notes: グループワークはスキットの創作や練習を中心に例文を示した。

b リスニング   Listening

ア．オーディオ機器を使う Using audio equipment   (((• TRACK 05 05 •)))

1. （最初に）CD［DVD］を聞きましょう。	Listen to the CD [the DVD] (first).
2. メモを取らないで聞いてください。	Don't write anything down. Just listen.

Ⅳ 小中連携のためのヒント

3. CD［DVD］を聞いて繰り返しなさい。	Listen and repeat after the CD [the DVD].
4. CD［DVD］を聞きその内容を話してください。	Listen to the CD [the DVD] and tell me what it is about.
5. CD［DVD］を聞いて質問に答えなさい。	Listen to the CD [the DVD] and answer the questions.

イ．教師が音読して聞かせる　Teacher's reading aloud　(((・TRACK 05 06・)))

1. 本文を読むので聞いてください。	I'll read the text. Please listen.
2. その一節を2度読みます。最初はゆっくり、次は普通の速さです。	I'll read the passage twice, first slowly, and then at a natural speed.
3. これから読む一節を聞いてください。そのあとにいくつか質問をします。	Please listen to the passage I am going to read. I'll ask you several questions afterward.
4. ジョンソンさんと私はスキットを読みます。そのあとクラスの皆に何の話をしていたか伝えてください。	Mr. Johnson and I will read the skit. Tell the class afterward what we are talking about.
5. ジョンソンさん、クラスの皆に最初の段落［節］を読んでくれますか？	Mr. Johnson, would you read the first paragraph [passage] to the class?

Notes: 4 は ALT と教師がスキットを読む場合、5 は ALT にモデル・リーディングを依頼する場合。

ウ．作業を行わせる　Giving tasks

(((• TRACK 05 07 •)))

1. 7ページの写真を見なさい。10個のものの名前を言います。○印で囲み、それがどこにあるのか言いなさい。

   Look at the picture on page 7. I am going to give you the names of ten things. Circle them and tell me where they are.

2. インタビューを聞いて図を埋めなさい。

   Listen to the interviews and fill in the chart.

3. CDの指示に従って絵を描きなさい。注意深く聞いてください。

   Now you are going to draw a picture by listening to the directions on the CD. Listen carefully, please.

4. 録音された5つの演説を聞きなさい。すべて本当に話されたものです。何についての話かを言ってください。

   Listen to five recorded speeches. They are all real speeches. Tell me what they are about.

5. 天気予報を聞いて図を完成しなさい。パートナーと図を交換して同じかどうか見てください。

   Complete the chart by listening to the weather forecast. Then exchange your charts with your partner to see if they are the same.

6. CDを聞き、お話の内容を要約して言ってください。

   Listen to the CD and tell me briefly what the story is about.

7. 5つのメッセージを聞いて、誰に向けてのものか当ててください。

   Here are five messages. Listen and find out who(m) they are addressed to.

Notes: 1は絵の中のものを聞き取り、その位置を伝えるリスニングとスピーキングを合わせたタスクの指示。2はインタビューを聞いて図表を完成するタスク。3は指示に従って絵を描かせるもの。4は音声を聞き、何のことについて話されているか当てさせる。5は天気予報を聞き、チャートを完成させる。6は物語を聞いて要約させる。7はメッセージを聞いて誰に宛てたものであるか当てさせるタスク。

C スピーチ・討論　　　Speech and discussion

ア．意見を求める　Asking for opinions　((・TRACK 05 08・))

1. どう思いますか。 — What do you think?
2. あなたはそう思いますか。 — Do you think so?
3. あなたの考えを知りたいです。 — I want to know your opinion.
4. それをどう思うか言ってください。 — Tell me what you think about it.
5. 何か提案はありますか。 — Do you have any suggestions [proposals]?
6. この問題へのあなたの意見は？ — What's your view about this problem?
7. あなたのお考えを聞かせてください。 — Would you tell us your idea?
8. 彼女［彼］に同意しますか？ — Do you agree with her [him]?
9. この意見に賛成ですかそれとも反対ですか？ — Do you agree or disagree with this opinion?

イ．スピーチをさせる　Asking for speech　((・TRACK 05 09・))

1. 今から自己紹介の短いスピーチをします。10分あげます。簡単な下書きをしなさい。 — Now you are going to make a short speech to introduce yourself. I'll give you ten minutes. Please write your rough draft.
2. 次の授業でこのエッセイに関して短いスピーチをします。長すぎたり短すぎたりしないで、100語以内くらいにしてください。 — In the next class you are going to make a short speech about this essay. Don't make it too long or too short. Please write it in about 100 words.

3. 今日は雄太と真紀がスピーチをします。雄太、真紀、準備はいいですか？	Today Yuta and Maki are going to make their speeches. Yuta and Maki, are you ready?
4. スピーチをする時には紙を読み上げるのではなく、暗記しなければいけません。	In giving [delivering] your speech, don't read from the paper. You must memorize your speech.
5. スピーチをする時、全員に聞こえるよう十分大きな声で話しなさい。小さな弱々しい声のスピーチほど退屈なものはありません。	In delivering your speech, speak loudly enough so (that) everyone can hear you. Nothing is so boring as listening to quiet, weak speeches.　＊thatは口語では省略されることが多い
6. スピーチをする時には最初は導入、そして内容、結論を書きます。この３つは省略しません。	In making your speech, first write the introduction, then the body and the conclusion. Don't skip any of the three.

Notes: スピーチを始める場合の例なので比較的長めの例が多くなっている。

ウ．暗唱させる　Asking for recitation　　(((・TRACK 05 10 ・)))

1. 今日は暗唱の練習をします。	Today we are going to practice recitation.
2. こちらがあなたの暗唱する文[手紙、詩]です。	Here is the passage [the letter / the poem] you are going to recite.
3. これを書いた人の気持ちを理解するようにしましょう。	Try to understand the feelings of the person who wrote this.
4. これが書かれた状況を理解することが大切です。	It is important for you to understand the situation in which this was written.

5. 誰が何を言っているか、その人がなぜそう言ったか［どんなふうにそれを言ったか］を考えないといけません。	You must think who said what and why he [she] said so [and how he [she] said it].

Notes: 3～5は暗唱（レシテーション）のテクニックについて言及している。

エ．討論をさせる　Asking for discussion　(((• TRACK 05 11 •)))

1. 今日は討論をします。10人ずつグループになり、輪になって座ってくれますか。	We're going to have a discussion today. Make groups of ten, and sit in a circle, will you?
2. それぞれのグループで討論のリーダーと報告者を決めてください。	In each group, please select a discussion leader and a reporter.
3. 今日は大気汚染について討論します。これについてどれくらい知っていますか？	Today we are going to discuss air pollution. How much do you know about it?
4. 本日の討論の議題は日本における天然資源です。この地域にあるものの例をいくつかあげられますか？	The topic for today's discussion is natural resources in Japan. Can you give some examples of natural resources found in this district? [Can you name some natural resources found in this district?]
5. 最初に資源についてどんな問題があるかを分析しなければなりません。	First, you must analyze what problems we have with our resources.
6. そしてその原因を考え解決法を提案し、それらを評価していきます。	Then, you should think about their causes, propose solutions and evaluate each of them.

小中連携を意識した
タスク活動例

Tasks for Cooperation between Elementary and Junior High Schools

　平成 27 年現在、公立小学校の 5, 6 年生の外国語活動の時間には文字指導は積極的に行わないことになっている。一方、中学校では、小学校で使っていた *Hi, friends!* と、中学校での文字を取り入れた英語の授業の橋渡しをする「準備期間」を設けている場合が多い。小学校英語から中学校英語へのスムーズな移行は、大きな課題となっている。

　ここでは、既に小学校で音声でのみ学んだ英単語を文字で提示することで、単語の音声、意味、文字の相互関係の理解を助けるタスクを紹介する。タスクの基本的な流れは以下の通り。

小中連携を意識したタスクの基本的な流れ

音声による input ▶ 文字の導入 ▶ 音、文字、意味の相互理解 ▶ output で知識の確認

タスク活動例 ❶　英語で時間を聞き、英語で答える

関連する外国語活動　*Hi, friends! 2*, Lesson 6　What time do you get up?
時間の目安　グループ学習で 30 分
ねらいと指導のポイント

　Hi, friends! 2　What time do you get up? と関連する表現について、口頭でやりとりを行ったあと、文字を導入する。最終的に英単語を並べて、正しい英文を作成できることをめざす。タスクは「基本編」と「発展編」から構成されている。

活動の進め方──基本編

　Hi, friends! 2, Lesson 6 の学習内容を音声で確認したうえで、文字での理解をめざす。"What time do you get up?" と、1 から 12 までの数字を使って自分が起きる時間 (I get up at ...) を英語で言えるように練習する。次に、

このやりとりを文字で認識できるようにする。

教具
1. 1 から 12 までのフラッシュカード（グループの数分）：表に数字、裏に英語のつづりが書かれたもの
2. | What | time | do | you | get up | ? | I | get up | at | と書かれたカード（グループの数分）

指導の手順
① 1 から 12 までの数を表す英単語をフラッシュカードで提示し、一緒に発音しながら、1 から 12 までの数を英語で練習して、文字で確認する。
② "What time do you get up?" "I get up at seven." の表現を使ったモデル会話を聞きながら、文脈を理解する。

――――――――― モデル会話 ――――――――― ((TRACK 05 12))

Teacher: Hi, class. Let's talk about your daily life. What time do you get up, Shoko?
Shoko: I get up at seven. I eat breakfast at eight.
Teacher: What time do you get up, Nozomi?
Nozomi: Well, I get up at eight. I run to school every day.
Teacher: I see. How about you, Tomo?
Tomo: I get up at six. I am an early bird! I help my mom cook.
Teacher: How nice!

教師　皆さんこんにちは。皆さんの日常生活について話しましょう。翔子、何時に起きますか？
翔子　7 時に起きます。8 時に朝食を食べます。
教師　希美は何時に起きますか？
希美　ええと、8 時に起きます。毎日学校に走って行きます。
教師　なるほど。朋はどうですか？
朋　6 時に起きます。早起きなんです。母が料理するのを手伝います。
教師　すばらしい！

③ 教師が "What time do you get up?" と質問して、生徒が起きる時間を口頭で答える練習をする。7 時であれば "I get up at seven." と言えるよ

う練習する。
④ 教師が "What time do you get up?" を文字で表したカードを提示して、意味を理解させる。
⑤ グループになる。教師がカードで「何時に起きるか」I get up at ... の英語を提示し、生徒は I get up at ...（〜時に起きます）とカードを正しく並べ替える。
⑥ グループの生徒同士で "What time do you get up?" "I get up at ..." のやりとりを口頭練習する。
⑦ グループで、一人の生徒が "What time do you get up?" を文字で提示しながら口頭で質問し、他の生徒が、何時に起きるかその時間を英単語カードで表しながら口頭で答える。

活動の進め方——応用編

"What time do you eat breakfast?" "What time do you go to school?" "What time do you go home?" など、get up 以外の動詞でも質問の意味がわかるようになることをめざす。

教 具
1. 1 から 12 までの数を表す英単語の書かれたフラッシュカード
2. What | time | do | you | get up | ? | I | get up | at | go | to | school | home | eat | dinner | breakfast | lunch | to | bed | が書かれたカード
3. 動詞（句）を表す絵カード
4. 時計を表す模型（または絵）
5. 質問紙（生徒に配布する）

指導の手順
① 教師は「学校へ行く」"go to school"「学校から帰宅する」"go home" の意味を表す絵と、それぞれを表す動詞（句）を文字で提示して、生徒と一緒に発音する。

②　時計の模型を黒板に貼り、教師が "What time do you go to school?" "What time do you go home?" などと質問する。生徒に黒板に貼ってある時計で時間を示させたあと、教師はその時間を英語で表現する。

　たとえば "What time do you go to school?" に対し、生徒が朝7時と黒板の時計で示せば "OK, you go to school at seven." と言う。このやりとりをクラスで繰り返し練習する。

③　教師は、生徒とともに "get up" "eat breakfast" "go to school" "eat lunch" "go home" "eat dinner" "go to bed" などの動詞句を発音練習しながら、文字で確認する。

④　ペアになり、生徒同士で1日のスケジュールを尋ね合う。ペアの生徒のスケジュールを英語で質問し、聞いた時間を下記の質問紙に書く。

―――――――― 質問紙の例 ――――――――

My friend *Masao's* daily schedule

1. He gets up at ＿＿＿＿＿.
2. He eats breakfast at ＿＿＿＿＿.
3. He goes to school at ＿＿＿＿＿.
4. He eats lunch at ＿＿＿＿＿.
5. He goes home at ＿＿＿＿＿.
6. He eats dinner at ＿＿＿＿＿.
7. He goes to bed at ＿＿＿＿＿.

選択肢：
one, two, three, four, five, six, seven, eight, nine, ten, eleven, twelve

　上記以外にも、"What time do you play basketball?" "What time do you take a bath?" "What time do you watch TV?" などの英語表現を入れてもよい。

指導のポイント

①　数字は1から12まで扱う。生徒が必要とする場合には、15 (fifteen)、30 (thirty) を教える。

② 英文を口頭で練習し、音声を認識したあと、それを表す英文を認識できるようにする。
③ 基本となる文（What time do you get up?）を教える時には、それが使われている場面を表したモデル会話を提示して、文脈を理解させる。
④ タスクは、生徒が実際の生活で経験するような場面で練習できるものを与える。
⑤ 大文字と小文字の違いにも注目させながら、音と文字の関係を理解させる。
⑥ 文字を書くことは中学1年では難しいので、リストから選んで、その英語を写すレベルにとどめる。

タスク活動例 ❷ 学校の周辺にある店を英語で言う

関連する外国語活動　*Hi, friends! 1&2*、中学校の検定教科書で扱う単語
時間の目安　ペア学習で20分
ねらいと指導のポイント
　学校の周辺にある店の名前を英語で確認したあと、文字で理解することをめざす。
　外来語として日本語で使われている語と英語の違いにも留意しながら、学校周辺にある店を英語で何というか理解させる。

活動の進め方

教具

1. 表に学校周辺にある店を表した英単語、裏に日本語が書かれたフラッシュカード（ペアの数分）
    例：bookstore（本屋）/ convenience store（コンビニ）/ hospital（病院）/ friend's house（友人の家）/ park（公園）/ post office（郵便局）/ restaurant（レストラン）/ school（学校）/ ... station（〜駅）/ supermarket（スーパー）/ small store(s)（小さい商店）/ temple（寺）
2. それぞれの店を表す絵カード（ペアの数分）
3. 街の地図（ペアの数分）

指導の手順

① 生徒に建物の絵を見せて、英語で何というか、フラッシュカードを使って文字を提示しながら教える。その後、教師は生徒に絵を示して "What's this?" と尋ねる。生徒は英語で答える。たとえば "It's a hospital." となる。

② 街の地図と建物の絵を使ってペアワークを行う。まず生徒がいつも学校へ行く途中に目にする建物の絵を地図の上に置かせる。次に、一方の生徒が絵を指さしながら、"What's this?" と尋ね、もう一方の生徒が "It is a ..." と、やりとりする。尋ねた生徒はその建物を表す英単語のカードを選び "I see. It is a ..." と復唱する。

会話例

((• TRACK 05 13 •))

Masato:（コンビニの絵を指さしながら）What's this?
Karin: It is a convenience store.
Masato:（convenience store のカードを選び）I see. It is a convenience store.

雅人　これは何ですか？
花梨　それはコンビニです。
雅人　なるほど。コンビニと言うのですね。

指導のポイント

① 学校の周りにある建物を英語で何と言うか興味を持たせる。
② 建物を表す英単語の意味、発音、文字の相互関係を理解させるために、絵と単語が書かれたカードを使って、生徒がこれらの相互関係を確認できるようなタスクにする。
③ 英単語を教える際に、外来語として入っている単語と比較して、違いに気づかせる。

小タスク活動例 ❶ 英語でクイズに挑戦！スリーヒント・クイズ

ここからは、小中連携を意識した小タスク活動、および教室英語の例を紹介する。授業始めのウォームアップ、授業終わりのクールダウン、授業中のブレイクなど、時間の枠やテーマの枠を超えて、いつでも使えて便利な活動である。

小学校における外国語活動と関連した小タスク活動を行うことで、生徒は中学校英語と外国語活動のつながりを認識する。それによって中学校英語への不安が軽減され、安心感が生まれる。また、生徒の英語への自信にもつながっていく。

関連する外国語活動　*Hi, friends! 1*, Lesson 7　What's this?「クイズ大会をしよう」
時間の目安　約3分
指導の手順　教師がクイズの答えのヒントを3つ出し、生徒が答える。
指導のポイント　既習の語彙を用いる、わかりにくい表現はジェスチャーを用いるなど生徒の実態に応じて工夫し、理解しやすいヒントを与える。

教室英語の例

TRACK 05 14

教師	では、クイズを出します！	Now, it's quiz time!
	What's this? クイズです。	It's "What's this?" quiz.
	ヒントは3つです。	I'll give you three hints.
	1番目のヒント。「赤と白」。	Hint No.1. It's red and white.
	2番目のヒント。「赤は丸い」。	Hint No.2. It has a red circle.
	3番目のヒント。「旗」。	Hint No.3. It's a flag.
	さぁ、何でしょう？	What's this?
生徒	…日本の国旗？	... A Japanese flag?
教師	その通り！　よくできましたね！	That's right! Good job!

小タスク活動例 ❷ **英語で時間割を言ってみよう！**

関連する外国語活動 *Hi, friends! 1*, Lesson 8　I study Japanese.「『夢の時間割』を作ろう」

時間の目安　約3分

指導の手順　クラスの時間割について、教師が英語で問いかけ、生徒が答える。

指導のポイント　既習の語彙を中心に用いて、適宜ヒントを与えるなど生徒の実態に応じながら答えを促す。

教室英語の例

((• TRACK 05 15 •))

教師	今日の時間割を、1時間目から順番に英語で言いましょう。	Let's say today's time schedule starting from the first period in English.
生徒	国語、理科、英語、体育…	Japanese, science, English, PE, ...
教師	5時間目は数学です。英語で何と言いますか？	The fifth period is *Sugaku*. How do you say it in English?
	Ma, ma... 当ててみて。	Ma, ma, ...Can you guess? [Try to guess.]
生徒	Math（数学）だ！	Math!
教師	よくわかったね！	Great!
	では、給食は英語で何と言う？	Then, how do you say *Kyushoku* in English?
生徒	Lunch（給食）だよね！ それは知っています。	Lunch! I know the word. ＊school lunch(es)とも言う
教師	正解！ 給食はよく覚えているね。	That's correct! You remember "lunch" well.

小中連携を意識した指導のポイント

　小中連携を意識した指導では、いかに小学校と中学校の間にギャップ、いわゆる「中1ギャップ」を作らないかが肝要である。中学校英語の入門期は、小学校における外国語活動の成果を中学校英語へつなぐ大事な時期である。小中連携を意識しながら授業を進め、英語に対する不安・抵抗感をなくして自信をもたせ、意欲を高めていきたい。以下の3つのポイントに注意しながら進めよう。

①　小学校で用いる教室英語、語彙、表現を使う

　外国語活動で使われる教材 Hi, friends! 1, 2（文部科学省、2012 a）と『Hi, friends! 1, 2 指導編』（文部科学省、2012 b）などを参考に、小学校で触れた語彙や表現を用いて、小学校の英語の授業を思い出すよう促す。小学校英語と中学校英語は異なるものではなく、結びついているものだと気づかせることが大切である。

②　ジェスチャーをふんだんに使い、理解の助けに

　外国語活動では、ジェスチャーや顔の表情を用いるコミュニケーションの大切さについて学習する（Hi, friends! 1 Lesson 2　I'm happy.）。ジェスチャーは言葉を理解する助けにもなるため、積極的に活用したい。

③　シンプルな表現で話す

　教師は生徒の「わかった！」という気持ちを大切にしたい。それが英語への自信につながる。教師は丁寧に指導したい思いから、説明しがちになることが多い。しかし、まずは生徒が理解できることを優先し、なるべく3～5語程度のシンプルな表現を心がけたい。

参考文献
文部科学省（2012 a）Hi, friends! 1, 2　東京書籍.
文部科学省（2012 b）『Hi, friends! 1, 2 指導編』東京書籍.

編者紹介

高梨庸雄（たかなし　つねお）
弘前大学名誉教授。ハワイ大学大学院修了。高等学校教諭、青森県教育センター指導主事、弘前大学教授を経て現職。全国英語教育学会・小学校英語教育学会・日英英語教育学会各顧問。編著書に『教室英語活用事典』（共編）、『英語リーディング指導の基礎』（共著）、『英語コミュニケーションの指導』（共著）、『英語リーディング事典』（共編、以上、研究社）、『「英語の読み書き」を見直す』（共著、金星堂）、『英語の「授業力」を高めるために』（編、三省堂）、『小学校英語から中学校英語への架け橋――文字教育を取り入れた指導法モデルと教材モデルの開発研究』（共著、朝日出版社）、『英語教材を活かす――理論から実践へ』（共著、朝日出版社）など。

小野尚美（おの　なおみ）
成蹊大学文学部英語英米文学科教授。インディアナ大学大学院修了。学術博士。昭和女子大学短期大学部を経て、2004年から現職。著書に『「英語の読み書き」を見直す』（共著、金星堂）、『ビジネスに成功する英文レター書式と文例――プレスリリース・請求書から契約書・研究報告まで』（共著、日興企画）、『言語科学の百科事典』（共著、丸善株式会社）、『英語の「授業力」を高めるために』（共著、三省堂）、『小学校英語から中学校英語への架け橋――文字教育を取り入れた指導法モデルと教材モデルの開発研究』（共著、朝日出版社）、『英語教材を活かす――理論から実践へ』（共著、朝日出版社）など。

土屋佳雅里（つちや　かがり）
東京成徳大学子ども学部助教、早稲田大学（非）、東京女子大学（非）。東京都杉並区立小英語講師。J-SHINE トレーナーとして、教員・指導者研修を行う。最近の著書は、『小学校はじめてセット』（執筆協力、アルク）、『先生のための小学校英語の知恵袋――現場の『?』に困らないために』（共著、くろしお出版）、『小学校教室英語ハンドブック』（共著、光村図書）、文科省検定教科書『Here We Go!』（光村図書）など。

田縁眞弓（たぶち　まゆみ）
京都光華女子大学こども教育学部教授。共著に『新編小学校英語教育法入門』『小学校英語内容論入門』（以上、研究社）、『小学校で英語を教えるためのミニマム・エッセンシャルズ』『小学校英語　だれでもできる英語の音と文字の指導』、文科省検定教科書『Crown Jr.』（以上、三省堂）など。

英文校閲
Carolyn Ashizawa

編集協力
望月羔子

音声吹き込み
Peter Serafin, Xanthe Smith

教室英語ハンドブック
きょうしつえいご

2016 年 2 月 1 日　初版発行
2023 年 9 月 8 日　4 刷発行

編者
高梨庸雄・小野尚美
たかなしつねお　おのなおみ
土屋佳雅里・田縁眞弓
つちやかがり　たぶちまゆみ

©T. Takanashi, N. Ono, K. Tsuchiya, M. Tabuchi, 2016

KENKYUSHA
〈検印省略〉

発行者
吉田尚志

発行所
株式会社　研 究 社
〒102-8152　東京都千代田区富士見 2-11-3
電話　営業 03-3288-7777（代）　編集 03-3288-7711（代）
振替　00150-9-26710
https://www.kenkyusha.co.jp/

装幀
Malpu Design（清水良洋）

本文デザイン・組版・本文イラスト
株式会社インフォルム

音声編集・製作
株式会社東京録音

印刷所
図書印刷株式会社

ISBN978-4-327-41092-6　C2082　Printed in Japan

研究社の出版案内

教室英語活用事典 改訂版

高梨庸雄、高橋正夫、カール・アダムズ、久埜百合〔編〕

小学校から大学まで、英語で授業を行う際に必要な英語表現を網羅したハンドブック。

英語で授業を行う際に必要な英語表現(クラスルーム・イングリッシュ)を、授業展開に沿って、場面別に収録したハンドブック。生徒とのやりとりの例や ALT との対話例も紹介。改訂にあたっては、表現をより実践的で使いやすいものに改めた。

目次
- 序　　小学校での教室英語
- 第1部　一般的指示
- 第2部　授業展開
- 第3部　授業のバリエーションとテスト
- 第4部　ALT との対話
- 第5部　教室英語歳時記

A5判 上製 388頁　ISBN 978-4-327-46149-2　C3082